The Big Book of Revenge

The Big Book of Revenge

200 Dirty Tricks for Those Who Are Serious About Getting Even

George Hayduke

Citadel Press
Kensington Publishing Corp.
www.kensingtonbooks.com

CITADEL PRESS books are published by

Kensington Publishing Corp.
850 Third Avenue
New York, NY 10022

All Kensington titles, imprints, and distributed lines are available at special quantity discounts for bulk purchases for sales promotions, premiums, fund raising, educational, or institutional use. Special book excerpts or customized printings can also be created to fit specific needs. For details, write or phone the office of the Kensington special sales manager: Kensington Publishing Corp., 850 Third Avenue, New York, NY 10022, attn: Special Sales Department, phone 1-800-221-2647.

Citadel Press logo Reg. U.S. Patent and Trademark Office
Citadel Press is a trademark of Kensington Publishing Corp.

First printing: February 2001

10 9 8 7 6 5 4 3 2

Printed in the United States of America

Library of Congress Cataloging-in-Publication Data

Hayduke, George
The big book of revenge : 200 dirty tricks for those who are
serious about getting even / George Hayduke.
        p.   cm.
Portions of this book have appeared previously in the author's:
Get even. [1980], ©1979; Get even 2. © 1981; and Revenge. © 1982.
"A Citadel Press book."
ISBN 0-8065-2141-4 (pbk.)
1. Revenge—Humor. I. Title.
    PN6231.R45H36   1999
818′.5402—dc21   99-41208
                CIP

Contents

General Advice

Throughout this book, I make many references to the mark, which is a street label hung on the victim of a scam or con. In our case, the mark is a bureaucrat, civil servant, lawyer, cop, businessperson, military officer, government official, teacher, merchant, manager, employer, employee, or other person who has done something unpleasant to you, your family, your property, or your friends. Never think of a mark as the victim of dirty tricks. Think of the mark as a very deserving target.

Before you read any of the specific areas of this book, please read these next few vital paragraphs. They tell how a trickster prepares before going into action.

1. PREPARE A PLAN.

Plan all details before you take any action at all. Don't even ad-lib something from this book without a plan of exactly what you're going to do and how. If your campaign involves a series of actions, make a chronological chart, then coordinate your efforts. Make a list of possible problems. Plan what you'll do if you get caught—depending upon who catches you. You must have every option, contingency, action, reaction, and evaluation planned in advance.

2. GATHER INTELLIGENCE.

Play like a real intelligence operative and compile a file on your mark. How detailed and thorough you are depends upon your plans for the mark. For a simple get-even number, you obviously need less intelligence than if you're planning an involved, time-release campaign. Before you start spying, make a written list of all the important things you need to know about the target—be it a person, a company, or an institution.

3. BUY AWAY FROM HOME.

Any supplies, materials, or services you need must be purchased away from where you live. Buy way in advance and pay in cash. Try to be as inconspicuous and colorless as possible. Don't talk unnecessarily with people. The best rule here—a good agent will get lost in a crowd of one. The idea is for people not to remember you.

4. NEVER TIP YOUR HAND.

Don't get cocky, cute, 'n' clever and start dropping hints about who's doing what to whom. I know that sounds stupid, but some would-be tricksters are gabby. Of course, in some of the cases this will not apply.

5. NEVER ADMIT ANYTHING.

If accused, act shocked, hurt, outraged, or amused, whichever seems most appropriate. Deny everything, unless, again, your plan involves overt personal involvement. If you're working covert, stay that way. The only cool badass out of Watergate was Gordon Liddy, and he kept his mouth shut.

6. NEVER APOLOGIZE; IT'S A SIGN OF WEAKNESS.

Normally, harassment of a citizen is a low-priority case with the police. The person's priority increases along with his socio-financial position in the community and with his political connections. If you are at war with a corporation, utility, or institution, that's a different ball game. They often have private security people, sometimes retired federal or state investigators. So by habit, these people may not play according to the law either. If you play dirty tricks upon a governmental body, be prepared to have a case opened. But how hard it is followed depends upon a lot of factors. Understanding all this ahead of time is part of your intelligence planning before you get started in action. The best advice I can offer is to know the law, know your rights, know the risks, weigh the risks, plan everything ahead of time in detail, be careful, and don't get caught. If you do get caught, don't admit anything to anyone...maybe not even to your lawyer. He may not want to know anyway.

This book has been simply organized by topical heading, which is by no means inclusive or even logical. You can use the table of contents as an index if you wish.

Disclaimer

The schemes presented in this book have been suggested by people who have actually used them. Many have asked to have their names changed or altered. Some have asked that I use totally fictional names. I did so to protect good people, maybe at the expense of bad people. However, the tricks, scams, stunts, cons, and scenarios presented here are given for *informational and amusement purposes only*. It is not my intent that you use this book as a manual or as a trickster's cookbook. I certainly don't expect that anyone who reads this book would actually ever do any of the things described here....

This book is written to entertain and inform readers, not to persuade them to commit an illegal act. I do not want to be responsible for the personal or corporate suffering of anyone, regardless of how deserved that suffering would be. There is a cynic's version of the Golden Rule that goes, "Do unto others as they have done unto you." Nastier cynics modify that to read, "Do unto others before they do unto you." Not being a cynic, I try to live by the real Golden Rule.

Additives

Harmful additives are a formidable weapon against machinery, people, and processes. Additives perform one or more of the following:

1. Corrosion...sulfuric acid, for example, will corrode the gutter, eaves, and downspout of a home; dumped salt will mar a building surface or floor and kill a lawn.

2. Contamination...copper salts will rot rubber products; soap in a public or corporate fountain will create giant foam. Or put it in a steam boiler if you're more serious about the matter.

3. Abrasion...introduction of light, coarse materials, such as resins, to automotive fuel, or metal filings placed in the gears of industrial machinery, will create frictional havoc.

4. Impurities...adding sugar to gasoline creates harmful carbon from the burning sugar, stopping the engine.

Soaps and detergents make wonderful additions to food and could even be beneficial if the target happens to be constipated. If not, then soap-laden munchies or drinks will really keep him moving.

During my stay as an invited guest of Uncle Sam I recall some dirty tricksters' making an action statement against being on KP. They liberally coated various pans and cooking vessels with GI soap. They washed mugs with a lot of soap, then neglected to rinse them before letting the utensils dry. Later, when some drinkable potion like milk or coffee was poured into the mug by some unsuspecting mark, the soap was activated. *Woosh!*

Soap is also a very effective additive to containers in which food is prepared. The secret is to disguise the taste. Various other additives will do that and other tricks.

A horny old pharmacist, Doctor Frank Pittlover, claims there really is a working aphrodisiac. His is almost as esoteric as the fake stuff you read about in men's magazines. Here's what Doctor Pittlover says: "It's known as yohimbine hydrochloride (C_{21}, H_{26}, O_3N_2), an obscure sex stimulant that operates on the central nervous system. It was the aphrodisiac used by the CIA in their MK/ULTRA scam." It is not on the Controlled Substances Act list—yet—and it is classed as a "veterinary aphrodisiac." That means you can get it openly from a pharmaceutical-supply source. What you do with it after you get it is probably your own business.

There are other references to and uses of additives in many other topical areas of this book...many more than could be indexed here.

"Take tea and see" is a good advertising slogan that should also alert the dirty trickster to some additives brought to our attention by herbal-tea producers. Two common products of many herbal teas have side effects that the true trickster could define only as delightful. First, some teas contain the leaves, flowers, and bark of the senna plant, a tropical shrub related to our bean plant. The dried leaves, bark, and flowers of this plant are a mighty powerful laxative. Chamomile flowers are also popular in herbal teas. Related to ragweed and goldenrod, chamomile can produce severe reactions in people sensitive to plants of that family.

The trick in both cases is to obtain extracts of both products and use them in concentrated enough additive form to create the desired effect.

Meanwhile, from the other end, Doctor Christopher

Garwood Doyle has a prescription that could really get a mark moving. Syrup of ipecac is a common purgative, easily available. Here's how Doctor Doyle uses it.

"Your mark is with you or your agent somewhere having a few drinks," the doctor outlines. "Presumably, the mark is drinking something sweet and heavy, like rum and Coke. When the mark goes to the bathroom or is otherwise out of the area, mix one tablespoon of syrup of ipecac in with the drink.

"You now have a fifteen-minute waiting—or escaping, if you prefer—period for the mixture to get active. After that, bombs away! The mark will begin violent projectile vomiting, which really messes up the nearby environment and anyone else who happens to be in the way.

"We first did this in medical school, using it to get back at a classmate who'd turned us in to officials for having an after-hours party in our dorm with women and booze. They threw the book at us because we were supposed to be mature medical students.

"The kid who did this fancied himself a real boozer," Doctor Doyle explained, "but he was a hell of a hypocrite about it and really played pious when he turned us in. So we figured he who tattles about booze shall also toss his booze."

Doctor Doyle reports that this additive will work easily with nonalcoholic drinks, too. He says the secret is to select a carrier drink that will hide the taste and consistency of the syrup.

Another good remedy for a hotshot is cascara sagrada, made from the dried root of a thorny shrub found on the American West Coast. It produces violent diarrhea. Once, Joe Kascaba introduced some cascara sagrada into a mark's orange juice. The mark was with his girlfriend and her parents in their family car. He had the "juiced" orange juice about ten minutes before getting into the car.

Kascaba reminisced, "The stuff's fast acting, and we were lucky to have the girlfriend's brother as our ally, to report the action. It hit the mark about six minutes into the trip, and in another minute he didn't even have time to yell for them to pull over. He just started letting go with loud, wet, explosive bursts.

"This is all in full witness of his girlfriend and her family in a tightly packed auto. He couldn't get stopped, either. They took him to a hospital, but by then the additive was through his system and the storm had subsided. That surely is super-powerful stuff."

Kascaba explained why he had taken this explosive action, saying, "The guy was a real creep. He was always trying to make out with other girls, and since he wasn't very smooth, he used to get them drunk. This was always with other girls, of course—his regular girlfriend knew nothing about all this.

"Well, one night he pulled this crap on a friend of mine, got her drunk, messed around...she got feeling all guilty and emotional, then got sick—puked, in fact. He thought he was macho stuff and gave her hell for it.

"We figured if he was going to act like such a shit...well, I'm sure you understand...."

As a final note, Kascaba says not to use this powerful additive with older folks, because it may weaken them to the point of very serious medical consequences.

The following trick is technically a substitution and not an additive: I know of one person who visited her mark's home and emptied the hair conditioner out of its bottle, then poured Neet hair remover into the conditioner bottle. She knew that her Operation Substitute was a bald success when she saw her mark in a local store several weeks later, wearing a large scarf on her head.

Vinegar makes a great substitute for nose drops or in nasal-spray devices. One especially nasty person also suggested it for use in eye drops. I'm not sure about that one, though. Sight's a precious thing.

Air Conditioners

In the interest of saving energy and being less self-indulgent, I am passing along this idea from Wilbur Aaron's brother. He says you can sabotage a window-mounted air conditioner with nothing more than a wad of chewing gum. The rationale for this is up to you, of course. I hope only that it's justified. Anyway, you simply stuff that wad of Wrigley's Best up the condensation drain tube of the unit. With luck your mark won't notice the overflow until his floor tiles lift off from the flooding moisture.

Air Polluters

This one's strictly for the minor league, neighborhood polluter, the small-timer whose smoky house chimney looks like the whole Indian nation is sending a smoke signal from his fireplace. Or try it on a small industrial plant where the roof and chimney stack have fairly easy access. Davey Jones dips into his nasty locker for an actual story.

"We had this neighbor who used to burn garbage in his fireplace. I think his specialty was burning old dead animals. The gunk that poured out of that man's chimney would give soot a good name. It made Gary, Indiana, look like God's country.

"The fallout, both particulate and odorous, was terrible all over the neighborhood. There were complaints to the authorities, petitions, neighborly persuasion visits. Nothing worked.

"Then, one night when he was out, we got up on his roof and poured soft tar down his chimney stack. He was gone two days, came back, and fired up his fireplace. After about ten minutes, the fiery heat ignited the soft tar coating we'd given his chimney . . . WHOOMM and WOOOSHHH, it looked like a combination of a Roman candle and a direct hit on a fuel dump in a war movie.

"The fire company got there in time to prevent serious damage, and the fire marshal gave him hell because of the situation. Everyone blamed the man for burning crap in there all those months. He moved out of the neighborhood shortly after that."

Airlines

Did an airline ever lose your luggage? Veteran air traveler Dottie Hunte suggests you return their favor and make yourself some money. Here's her scam. Arrange to have a friend meet you at the terminal gate when you deplane. Give your friend your baggage claim checks and have him/her retrieve your bags from the carousel, then leave the baggage area with your bags. Before your friend leaves the airport with the luggage, be sure you get your claim checks back. Then you saunter over to the baggage area and spend half an hour waiting for your bags. Ask some clerk for help, then report your "missing" luggage, showing your claim checks as proof.

"Very few flights ever have a clerk actually check the baggage and collect the claim checks," she says. "It's foolish, but they don't."

She suggests you "make a polite but firm scene and demand satisfaction. Normally, the airline people will have you fill out a form, and they will attempt to trace your luggage. Obviously, they won't find it. Bug them some...write them letters. Soon, you should get a good settlement from the airline." Don't pull this one on the same airline more than once, Hunte cautions.

Leaving the airlines and aiming for the individual mark, you can do a lot of personal damage. For instance, if you find that your mark is going to use airline travel and there are only a few travel agents in town, you could call until you find the correct one and cancel the reservations. Or if you know the name of the airline, call their office and cancel the mark's reservations.

You might try to slip a couple rounds of pistol ammunition or a switchblade knife into your mark's pocket just before he goes through the metal detector at the airport terminal. You could also slip some drugs into his pocket at the same time. Read a book on pickpocketing to note the technique for doing this. It's quite easy.

Bill Cutcheon sometimes poses as a Moonie, Hare Krishna devotee, or other cultist and goes to airports. His goal is to act a completely obnoxious fool. He really hams it up, usually getting tossed out after totally grossing out passengers. The heat, of course, falls equally on the cults and on the airport for letting "them" behave like that.

Another Cutcheon stunt is to leave accurate-looking but totally bogus hijack scenario plans, bomb diagrams, or orders of battle for terrorist attacks in airport bars and restrooms. This fires up both the rent-a-cops and the real security people. The security delays and resultant hassles with passengers create unhappy people who are angry at airports and airlines.

Naturally, the blame for these plans must focus on the original perpetrator of Cutcheon's problems. He says, "If some nut group's been hassling me for money, messing in my neighborhood, or otherwise being obnoxious, I'll leave evidence to pin the hijack or bomb rap on them. I got back at a motorcycle gang by doing this once, after they had sideswiped my truck and refused to pay damages."

He also explains that this is a good vengeance grabber against an airport facility that has offended you.

Mitch Egan of San Francisco doesn't like cultist panhandlers harassing people at airports, so he founded the Fellowship to Resist Organized Groups Involved in Exploitation, or FROGIE. Egan and his friends use those little metal clickers shaped like frogs to ward off religious solicitors.

According to Egan, thousands of people across the country

are now armed with the little metal frogs, and when a religious panhandler approaches, they whip out the clicker and *"Click, click, click!"* the pest away.

"In San Francisco, I saw two hundred people clicking away at a Krishna," Egan remarked. "They blew her right out of her socks."

He adds, "If God wants a dollar from me, he can ask for it. I'm not against religion, but I'm fed up with organized beggars.

Relief is just a click away.

I knew a chap who became annoyed at a Krishna who followed him out of the Indianapolis airport, verbally abusing him for not making a contribution. Having surreptitiously "armed and primed" himself, our hero suddenly stopped, whipped around, and peed all over the startled harridan. After the few necessary seconds of attack, he calmly replaced himself, zipped up, and walked away. A bemused security cop standing nearby tried to hide his laughter.

Animals

If your mark is an oily cuss with a credibility problem, you could easily pull off this stunt suggested by good old country boy Emil Connally. It involves a cop, reporters, SPCA folk, and some farm animals.

According to Connally, here's how it works. You have two marks. The prime one is a farm owner with the credibility problem. We'll call him Mr. Big. The secondary mark is a cop who's made an enemy of you. In this case, pick one of your local Attila the Hun cops, because he's a bully and his ego for a bust will get in the way of his grain-sized brain.

Call the cop—try for his home phone even if it's unlisted—and tell him you know about a cock or dog fight that's being held at Mr. Big's farm. Explain you have no morals against animal fighting (build your own macho image) but you lost big money the last time and you think the fights are fixed. Mention drugs and booze, too. Next, call Mr. Big and tell him you're an anonymous political ally who wants to warn him about some people holding dog or cock fights at his farm. Call reporters and the SPCA and tell them all about the fight. Tell them that Mr. Big and the cop have a payoff relationship. Give everyone the same general arrival time...never be too specific.

If all goes well, all will sort of show up at roughly the same time. You might manipulate things so the press and animal lovers show up first. Even if a real story doesn't develop, you have scattered some strong seeds of distrust.

There is a variation if you want a stronger story. Kill and mutilate a dog or rooster, then bury it several days before you set up your animal-fight scenario at Mr. Big's place. Tell the reporters and the SPCA where the evidence is buried. It will be fun to hear the two marks talk about these things to the other parties. Maybe there's a story here after all.

Dead animals are so useful. Don't you agree? A nefarious lady known only as Hong Kong Hattie once waited until her mark went to the airport to depart for a five-day business trip. Then, using the nefarious methods for which she is so famous, Hattie got to the mark's car in the airport parking lot and got the lock opened. She then stuffed a large and very dead groundhog into the glove compartment. Hattie locked the car and strolled away. Reportedly, the mark sold his car at quite a financial loss just a few days after getting back from his business trip.

One of the plagues for newspaper deliverers is barking, biting dogs that attack both kids and their bicycles. Tom Frickert, today a newspaper magnate but once a paperboy, has a solution.

"A good-quality plastic water pistol filled with freshly squeezed lemon juice is the ticket," Frickert says with a chuckle. "You shoot the felonious furball right in the eyes, and it'll soon stop the canine harassment.

"I once shot a big, nasty cur with the juice, and he never bothered me again...used to hide under his master's porch whenever I came down the sidewalk to deliver the newspaper.

If your neighbor's constantly yowling and howling dog bothers you, congratulations, you're normal. But unlike most who sit and suffer, you can call the local SPCA and tell them how the neighbor mistreats the animal. Hold your phone near the window so the SPCA official can hear the "evidence" right from the source.

Apartments

Here's a switch, a landlord seeking revenge against tenants. Rob Roosel claimed that the hippies he rented to were tearing up his place. He tried the entire law book of legal ways to get back, all without success. So, he waited until he finally had these obnoxious tenants exterminated from his place by virtue of the lease expiring. He made very sure he knew where the tribe had moved. Happily, they bought a small house of their own in another neighborhood. Roosel smiled.

He explained, "I got a few yards of rubber tubing from a science supply store, attached it to a large funnel, drank about 27 beers, then visited their Hippie Heaven. I slipped the tubing under their door and offloaded all that beer-fed urine into the funnel. I did that every night for four days. When I came back on the fifth night I noticed they had put in a porch light and had a 'Beware of Dog' sign in the yard."

Roosel added, "Hee Hee Hee."

If you don't like beer 'n' urine, then hold the onions for your mark's abode. That is, you can bury onions inside flowerpots, particulary those near heaters or radiators in the wintertime. The stench soon becomes overpowering, but is unlocatable.

John P. Neal offers another suggestion for the new miracle glues as a household weapon. He had a landlord who was an absolute waste when it came to doing anything about the lack of heat in the apartment. John was freezing. After getting nowhere on his last complaint, John gave notice and was moving out. When he went to the landlord's home to get back his security deposit, he had a friend, by prearranged time signal, call the landlord on the telephone—in another room. Quickly, John went to the landlord's thermostat, turned it to its maximum, then used quick drying Super-Glue to lock the controls at that setting. He also put glue on the screws which gave access to the instrument. Finally, he put a glue seal around the device and the wall. He heard that the landlord had to use a wrecking bar to pry the thermostat off the wall and a furnace man had to come to put things right.

The landlord tried to sue John, but had no proof. He should have known better. If justice really worked, we wouldn't need books like this, would we?

Old timer trapper Zeb Porkmore got stung by a fast-talking salesman who ripped him off by leasing him a horrible apartment. Zeb tracked the real estate scoundrel to his own place. Then, he did his intelligence gathering homework. He tells the rest of his story.

"You know about those liquid room fresheners that come in small bottles? I have the reverse of that in mind. I got a one ounce bottle of animal trapping lure. Some of these lures are the ugliest smelling crap known in the civilized world. Most are made of ground-up unmentionable glands mixed in with some of the dead animal's urine. The whole mess is allowed to putrify. Only a few drops will attract other animals to traps or whatever.

"What is wonderful is that only a few drops are also enough to turn the stomach of even the most case-hardened mortician. A few drops of any of these lures in your mark's apartment will instantly sicken your target. There is no known way to get rid of the stink for a few days."

I also figured the same stuff would work in a car, an elevator, a conference room, a courtroom or on the mark's clothing. On second thought, why not use it on the mark himself? If your mark behaves like an uncivilized animal, then he or she should smell like one, too.

A refinement to the exploding apartment light fixture I explained in the first book, whereby you tape a bag of fresh feces loaded with an explosive charge and wired to the mark's light switch in his or her room, came from Chris Loop. He suggests you substitute a payload of fresh worms, small dead animals, raw sewage, vomit, paint, urine, or a combination of any of the above.

Auto Dealers

If an automobile dealership screws you, on either the car, the deal, or the service, don't get angry—get even. Wait outside the showroom until a prospective customer starts talking to a salesperson about the same type of car you got. Walk right up to the customer and tell your woeful story. The idea is to screw up as many sales as you can. Be factual, be cool, and act as if you're an honest citizen trying to save another honest citizen some money and heartache—as you wish someone had done for you. Sincere good faith is the thing here, because the salesman is going to blow his about the second time you pull your act.

When the manager asks you to leave and you don't, he will probably call the police. You had anticipated this earlier and alerted someone at the local newspaper or television station—probably the action-line reporters. Smalltown media usually won't allow reporters to come—car dealers buy lots of ads, and you don't. A regional TV station may show up—if you promise a confrontation with the law. So when the manager calls the police, you call your TV reporter—fun and games for the 6:00 P.M. news.

If all this doesn't work, wait off the dealer's premises and approach customers as they leave the showroom. Tell your story there and then. Offer to help them avoid your mistake. But stay on public property. And keep after the action-line reporters.

If you want to escalate the attack a bit, show up when the night salespeople are on duty—they won't recognize you. Look at new cars; wander around. Few salespeople pay much attention to an obvious gawker. As soon as someone else or a telephone distracts the salesperson, you can do things to the automobile right there in the showroom. A bottle opener is hard on the finish. See the section on additives for things you could quickly put into the fuel tank. If you could smuggle some in with you, stuff roadkill under a car seat or in the glove compartment. Or toss a condom (preferably used) on the front seat. By the way, used condoms make wonderful plants in other locations as well, like the boss's desk, or in a customer's car back in the service shop.

If you can manage to slip undetected into the service area along with your bag of sabotage goodies, such as glue, wire cutters, paint, potatoes, M80s, etc., you can run amok. Work quietly and quickly. This sort of guerrilla warfare can literally wreck a dealer's service reputation.

Automobiles

Many camheads and antivehicular guerrillas must read my books, or else they are more prolific than the rest of you. Without fail, the heaviest amounts of mail come from readers who want to share nasty things you can do to automobiles. Many stunts were duplicated, and a few were totally without humor or redeeming revenge value, so they are not included here.

Maybe I should have named this book *Auto Madness.* It seems everyone has something nasty to do to every mark's car. E.W. from Hastings (a funny name), Nebraska, is a perfect example of motoring meanness. He writes, "George, try dropping a handful of BBs or lead shot down the carburetor of your mark's car . . . big, big, big repair bills."

Next, E.W. wants you to drain the oil from the mark's automobile. Replace the plug, then fill the crankcase with water. He says this will do more damage than simply letting the oil run out. E.W. says this works well because the oil warning lamp will not come on, yet the engine doesn't have any oil—which it needs so badly. Wasn't it in the Bible where I read that oil and water don't mix?

I'm sure all you motorheads and straights enjoyed the scene in *American Graffiti* where Officer Holstein has the rear end ripped out from under his cruiser. The movie is history, but modern technology now makes it easier than ever to recreate that scene for real. It works for any mark, not just those of the law enforcement persuasion.

Our Kansas City whiz, Jimi the Z, cautions that you do this to nobody but a truly mortal foe because it is so devastatingly expensive.

"You need some quarter-inch Kevlar rope, which is fairly lightweight, almost invisible at night, but stronger than hell. Attach one end around both axle sides with a double half-hitch. Leave twenty-five feet or so of slack, then attach the other end to a cement post, steel lightpole, or something that isn't going anywhere when the vehicle tries to.

"Believe me, this is fantastic to watch, to see the results. It almost always totals the car, as the entire rear end suspension is destroyed with great frame damage as well," Jimi writes with glee.

Meanwhile, there is more to fuel the imagination. Herb Bobwander is a real sweetie when it comes to sugaring your mark's gas tank. He says, "Sugar itself is messy and hard to pour into a tank. That's why I always use sugar cubes. Just a few in the old gas tank, and his MPG will drop to zilch, his car will stall out all the time and behave like a lemon-colored dog." Gee, Herb, you sound just like a commercial . . . for Hayduking a car.

If your mark has given you gas pains or a bellyache and you have access to his car, let's next add Sam Stein's fuel to the fires of your revenge. Sam says to take your hacksaw and cut off about three inches of the pipe leading to the car's gas tank.

"Do it a few inches from the top of the tank so all the gas doesn't spill out. Also, leave at least six inches of pipe connected to the gas tank well opening at the car body.

"Take a length of black plastic tubing about three feet long, attach it to the upper pipe, and secure it with a clamp. Run the rest of it down under the car so the end points to the right of the car. Secure this under the car with wires and string. Then, cut the tubing about six inches from the side of the car, so nobody will spot it."

Sam says that when the mark goes into the gas station to fill 'er up, he's in for a surprise. As most gas jockeys just lock the nozzle

and walk away, thinking it will automatically stop . . .
well . . . there should be about fifty dollars of gasoline on the
ground before anyone realizes something is wrong.

On the other hand, if he just puts in a few dollars worth, the
mark may not notice the puddle from his misdirected gas supply
line and will soon run out of gas. Let's hope it's miles from the
nearest station.

Either the American Mothball Marketing Association or fifty
readers had the same idea. It seems that ten or fifteen mothballs
popped into an auto's gas tank does an amazing job of murdering
its engine. Unlike sugar, these little timebombs dissolve
completely in gasoline, so there is no visible evidence. This one
sounds like big bills at the repair shop.

If you place a judicious amount of plaster of Paris in someone's
automobile carburetor it will at least keep the butterfly valve
open and that's at the very least, says Elmo Lang of Zanesville, Ohio.

This idea is untried but seems chemically sure, according to
Alexander Hogg of Tampa. He says that an ordinary Tampax
stuffed into a diesel fuel tank will dissolve into extremely fine
fibers which will clog filters and injection pumps. It seems as if
that would be a bloody nuisance to the engine's owner.

Putting additives in the crankcase is old hat. Instead, put things
in with the transmission fluid. If the mark's car is an automatic,
many of the fuel and oil additives mentioned in the earlier books
will also destroy the transmission. Or, as Todd Proudfoot
advocates, you can dissolve a bit of paraffin wax in ethlene glycol.
It will stop any auto transmission.

Wilson R. Drew provided two very positive and negative
numbers to be used for your mark's automobile. His first idea is
to switch the No. 1 and No. 8 wires in the firing order on the
distributor cap of a vehicle with an automatic transmission. You
will find these wires marked by number. This will allow the
vehicle to start either in "Neutral" or "Park" positions, but will
kill the engine as soon as the shift lever is put into "Drive." It will

happen repeatedly and cause all sorts of expensively fun problems for the mark, and profit for some mechanic.

Mr. Drew's second idea involves people who want to touch your car, such as hoodlums, thieves, and other street scum that you want to keep away. Get a coil from a Ford Model A car and have it hooked up by a competent and friendly mechanic. He hooks it to your car in such a way as to discourage the street slime from touching live metal surfaces. According to Mr. Drew, if this is done properly, whenever any unauthorized person touches the door handles, bumper, or hood latch, he will receive a jolt of electricity that feels like a right cross to the genitals. A small toggle switch located beneath the car will shut off the electricity whenever you wish.

I also got a lot of auto-related letters from people who are furious with the idiotic way drivers behave in shopping center parking lots. I agree. Parking in handicapped zones, fire lanes, walkways, and in front of stores is boorish, lazy, inconsiderate, and downright deserving of all sorts of Haydukian mayhem.

Pud Drunchniak tells me that he cruises the mall lots until he spots a repeat offender he has noted from before. Pud is retired, you see, and has a lot of time to help make our world more civilized.

"I see these uncivilized, healthy louts parked where they shouldn't be while some senior citizen or mother with her little kids has to hike through a hundred yards of slush from her spot in the parking lot to get to the store. That isn't right, and I do something about it."

Old vigilante Pud carries a Crossman air pistol and a WHAMO wrist rocket with an ample supply of ammo for both in his car. He parks with a clear shot at the offending vehicle well within range and fires several rounds at the vehicle, wounding its windows or finish.

"I wait until there is noise or something else distracting before I take action, of course," Pud advises. "Sometimes I work only at night. I make two or three attacks on different targets from different locations and positions, then I leave the mall for the day.

Once in awhile I work from the mall roof, too. But, I'm not as young and mobile as I used to be, so I mostly stick with my car."

That spring-loaded prick punch that machinists use is a handy pocket tool and quite aptly named for dealing with marks. With reasonable quietness, it will punch a few neat holes in the body panels of the mark's car, showing him where you think he should mount a few do-dads from Western Auto, or so says Texas's R.W.

Here's one that almost seems timid, as if the meek really have taken over the earth. It's another variation on how to get back at some lout who bangs his car door into your car at some parking facility. You just stick toothpicks in any and all locks on the mark's car, then break them off in the lock. It helps if it's winter and the toothpick is wet. Actually, this stunt will work in almost any lock.

Jimi the Z doesn't believe in just slashing tires. He says to use pliers and pull out the stems. But, he tells you to leave the stems there as it is a riot to watch marks try to stuff them back in. Jimi suggests this great payback for subhuman slimeballs, e.g., those rude bastards who steal handicapped parking spots.

Meanwhile, moving inside the vehicle, you've heard of bees in your bonnet? With apologies to our British cousins, David Muridae has a little surprise for your mark's automobile glove box. Our Illinois-based trickster suggests loosing a container full of bees or wasps into the glove box. The poor mark will bumble into that lot and learn what a sting operation is really like.

California's infamous Arlo Jones has a lot of splendid suggestions to help you modify your mark's automobile. For instance, if your mark's vehicle has power seats, move the seat into a totally uncomfortable position, then cut the power cable that controls movement, or superglue the control knob.

According to Arlo, you can also easily create an ant farm on wheels with the mark's car by removing the ashtrays in the rear seat armrests. You'll find a lot of space under there for you to stuff half-eaten hamburgers or roadkill, then dump a can of soda on that mess. You could also produce the start of an ant culture by picking up a few strays from the sidewalk and introducing them to their new home. Replace the ashtray and wait. Arlo also mentions that if your mark's car features hidden windshield wipers, removing them will create quite a shock next time your mark is out driving in the rain or snow.

If you like syringes of all sizes, Filthy McNasty, our resident expert on various forms of antiestablishment guerrilla warefare, also has some tactics to try on your mark's car. He says to fill a basting syringe with castor oil, then squirt it into the tailpipe and muffler of the mark's car. After a few minutes on the road, the vehicle will start to smoke beyond belief.

You can also use this syringe to squirt a good dose of formaldehyde, el tacko perfume, vile urine, or whatever else through the mark's car's open window. Or, crack the window, run a garden hose in, and flood his car for real.

Jimi the Z is full of more ideas. This time he wants to reprogram the mark's custom car horn—the type where the owner records his own tune onto the little keyboard or cassette recorder. Here's the new idea. Substitute some of your really gross stuff for his original selection. For example, among some Latins, the familiar refrain "Shave and a Haircut, Two Bits," is interpreted as meaning, "Screw Your Mother." This meaning was independently confirmed by an East L.A. friend of mine.

I surely brought out all the experts of the automobile sabotage trade. Jerald Jordan adds an improvement to the old trick of supergluing car locks by telling us that you can also use that famous glue to seal the door's weather stripping to the car body. Just apply the glue all the way around and slam the door.

If you'd like the police to stop his car and speak with your mark, you can attract their attention by disconnecting his rear turn signal lights or his rear car lights. Sam from Connecticut did this to a habitually drunken fellow employee who was a menace on the road. Sam wanted the police to nail him for drunk driving. He got police attention by removing the bulbs from the aforementioned drunk's car lights, causing police to pull the heavily marinated mark over. Result: a free trip to jail for the sot, plus a heavy fine.

Bars

A lot of women won't go into bars alone because derelicts of all persuasions will bug them. Some guys report that these creeps hit on their dates even with them present. What's this world coming to? Anyway, one young lady found a scam to strike back at these score-artists. Her name is Wanda Woodland, and here's her method.

"I like to have a few drinks without all sorts of creeps bothering me. But, it never works out that way. I decided to make them as miserable as they made me. So, one night, I let a guy buy me all kinds of drinks, and I ordered the most expensive stuff I could get. We then went through the 'ride home' ritual of stopping at a cocktail lounge with a motel. I had insisted we take my car which was O.K. with him. He didn't know it, but it was essential for my plan.

"His line was offered and I accepted. So far, I hadn't even had to kiss the jerk, and he hadn't tried to touch me. I let him pay for the motel room, and while he was in the shower getting all sexy, I took out my lipstick and wrote on the large mirror above the bed, "MY FUN WAS IN YOUR CHASE . . . START WITHOUT ME," quietly left the room, got in my car, and went home . . . laughing all the way."

Bathrooms

Hedley Herndon from L.A. has a good idea for any mark who displays an anal personality. He claims that he invited a guy to several parties and the man made a complete ass of himself with the ladies, food, and drink. Hedley thought payback was in order. He quietly walked into one of the mark's drunken parties and found a spare roll of toilet paper in the closet.

"I had some Tabasco sauce in a small spray bottle. I didn't want to hurt anyone at the party, so I unrolled some of the paper on the spare roll, then sprayed a few feet of it, let it dry, then rolled it back up again and put it back for him alone to use," Hedley relates.

Bathtubs

Just because a lot of good clean fun can happen in a bathtub if the right people are present doesn't mean dirty work can't be applied. Boswell G. Pendleton suggests that if you want to really roast your mark, you either place a copious amount—like two jars—of commercial meat tenderizer in his or her bathwater, or have an accomplice do it. According to Pendleton, it's much more fun if you can have a liberal-minded assistant do it, because of the entire scenario of social intercourse, dining foreplay, coy sparring, etc., etc., culminating in a "rich soaking bath" before the main event.

"It works well on any of the three sexes," Pendelton advises. "And, the surprise is wonderful. The best part is that the jerk in the tub actually starts to cook, as the tenderizer is a hell of an irritant. The discomfort alone is a totally adequate excuse to discontinue the evening. I heartily recommend this one."

From an expert like that, the endorsement stands on its own.

Moving up from the tub to the shower head, I saw a potentially good idea in the Goldie Hawn comedy film *Private Benjamin*. It involved getting back at a mark by packing the pipe or cavity behind the shower head with a concentrated solution of brightly colored dye. The mark hits the shower, hopefully with eyes shut, the water filters through the dye and hopefully transfers to the mark. It worked well in the film, which is, of course, par for

Hollywood.

In your interest I asked several domestic experts if this trick has any basis in reality. All said it did, but not to the dramatic extent of success in the film. But, all said it would work to varying degrees depending upon the amount and concentration of dye, color of dye, permanency of the solution, amount of time between placement and shower use, temperature and pressure of the water, etc. But, all did agree the basic plan would work. They suggested experimentation. I thought that sounded like a peachy keen idea, too. Maybe it's time you put your favorite showertime mark on a dyette.

Billboards

Check the *Graffiti* section, too, but for this chapter, I'm indebted to Gordon Goofbutt of Friendship, Maryland, for persuading some of his colleagues to do some creative captioning on local billboards. After painting over the existing advertising headlines, they inserted their own balloon/caption combinations. Gordon says most were gross and obscene, e.g., on one billboard showing a handsome couple smoking a well-known cigarette brand, the male is saying to the female, "Sit on my face, and I'll guess your weight."

Booze

As every dedicated alcholic knows, the prescription drug "Antabuse," which is really Disulfiram, will make a person dreadfully ill if taken with booze. The drug is prescribed for recovering alcoholics to insure that if they do slip off the wagon and take a drink, they will get sick as can be if they are also taking their Antabuse medication.

The reader who suggested this idea cautions that you should not mix the drug directly with alcohol. Get the drug into the mark some other way, prior to the ingestion of alcohol. The reader says the drug is not all that tough to get, despite being a prescription item. But it is much more potent than the Ipecac mentioned in our first volume. Be careful.

For some mysterious reason a number of my friends are truly hardcore beer drinkers. You know, the kind of guys who think an after dinner speech is a horrendous belch . . . ? Anyway, Norman Althree and his roommate Cricket Easter had these really bad neighbors who used to wander over, uninvited, and rip off pitcher after pitcher of draft beer during parties hosted by my friends. These freeloading swine never offered to even up, barter, or make any hospitable gesture.

Naturally, some gesture was in order by someone.

At the next soiree, when the cheapies showed up for their fifth refill, Norman had a special pitcher for them. By this time, the nefarious neighbors were enough sheets to the wind that they were hogging down anything that looked like beer.

Urine looks a lot like beer, expecially when it's fresh and has a good head on it. Mixing in a little beer can complete the disguise, Norman says.

Norman passed along another version in which beer that is four or five days stale and flat can be put into commercial apple juice bottles and distributed. He says, "You can give them to people like our now ex-neighbors or you sneak the bogus juice into their refrigerators. I guess you could use this same idea if you got angry enough at a supermarket.

"Just load up a few apple juice bottles with one of your substitutes and place it back on the shelf. Security people look for you sneaking food out of a store, but who looks for you sneaking in!"

He makes a point. Apple cider anyone?

Sheree West is a delightful mistress of mayhem whose good looks and petite appearance totally disguise her tough, rottenly evil sense of revenge. A lover of animals, she has been known to introduce mice and/or sparrows to the homey environment of her mark's automobile upholstery or the mark's home. She says, too, that mealworms may be dropped in cereal boxes, etc.

Her high-water mark to date, though, involved a besotted roommate who would stumble in obnoxiously drunk night after night, spilling all her life's sob-sister tragedies, as well as her evening's food and drink, all over the apartment.

Enough! Sheree waited until an expecially bad evening. She had personally seen her roommate inhale seven beers as her final consumption of that evening, then fall into her usual passout supine position in bed, all without visiting the bathroom to offload the used beer by-product.

Our lovely little nastiness carefully and deftly sewed her blottoed buddy's clothes shut, including the fly buttons on her pants. Sheree sewed her roommate's long blouse sleeves to her pants legs. Then, she sewed Dolly Drunk's blouse, slacks and socks to the bed. Finally, she placed the sad souse's hand in a bowl of warm water.

The mark started to get that desperate urge to answer nature's call and sort of woke up. But, she couldn't get mobile enough to leave her bed, no matter how hard she struggled. You can guess the rest, i.e., to reissue the coinage of Women's Lib slogan, "You can sleep in the wet spot tonight" when you're the mark and your fate is all sewed up.

Bounty Hunters

Look through the dozens of relatively recent "Wanted" posters in the post office for some nasty criminal who looks like your mark. Hopefully, your mark is not too well known or is a newcomer. According to J. Edgar Murtha, it's amazingly true that in checking two hundred or so posters you'll be able to come up with six people who have a fairly close resemblance to your various enemies or marks. Borrow these posters.

To put this plan into action, show your mark's poster (or use Xerox copies to which you've affixed a seal from your notary stamp—described in earlier books) around macho bars where amateur bounty hunters and other guys who read *Soldier of Fortune* hang out. Drop word that you're a pro hunter and that there's a $25,000 reward for this person. In hard times your wanted poster, and your mark, will attract a lot of attention. If you're especially ballsy, visit the local constables and show them the poster copies.

The thing that really makes this work, according to Murtha, is *also* showing some realistic stakeout-type photos of the subject which you have taken yourself. Explain that these are "surveillance" photos. Let your bounty hunter or constable compare the photos and the poster. The closer you get to the mark's neighborhood, the faster your operation will come home to haunt him.

Bumper Stickers

A simple refinement was suggested to permanentize unwanted bumper stickers that you place on your mark's auto. Be sure to use one of the new, modern glues over and under to insure the sticker will not be easily removed. That's gentle, compared to the next paragraph.

Although no sane person would literally endorse this idea, it's a hell of an attention getter, especially in a center city area. This time the message on your bumper sticker is a terse, KILL POLICE. Or, if you're squeamish, use MAIM POLICE. You get the idea. The one time I know of this being used was when someone placed it on the bumper of a city councilman who was a Stone Age era redneck with an IQ of just about room temperature. It upset his buddies at the cop house badly and they never quite trusted that councilman again. An unforgiving hippie waited a long time to get his partial revenge on that politician.

Bureaucrats

Bubba Bates was had by a buck-passing bureaucrat in Florida, i.e., he was screwed out of a good job by this paperwork parasite. Buck had an advertising inspiration. He placed an ad in local papers offering jobs to "Male Secretaries Only." He included such come-ons in the copy as "$11 an hour, must be physically attractive and gentle," plus a few more choice character traits. He then listed the mark's name and office location with a strong "no phone calls" admonition in the ad. He set the show-up-for-interview time as one half-hour prior to the mark's office actually opening. That meant that when the bureaucratic mark arrived at work on the morning in question, he had a lot of very ungentle male secretaries bitching away at each other and then at him for his cattle call style of recruitment. I'd be willing to bet that some members of the local vice squad were there, too. Bubba Bates says you can repeat this one as often and with as many variations as you feel the mark requires.

Butane Lighters

Early in 1980, the American news media sensationalized rumors of the horrible dangers of butane lighters. With their usual lack of checking for accuracy, they printed wild stories about accidental deaths caused by butane lighters exploding with the power of three sticks of dynamite. Sensing this to be nonsense, I contacted OSHA, The National Safety Council, and several other organizations to verify the claim. They turned out to be totally untrue.

However, butane lighters will explode if exposed to sparks, fire, or intense heat. One nasty type who used to do contract work for the CIA suggested, jokingly, of course, that a butane lighter be shoved into the tailpipe of your mark's car, then moved along with a stiff wire until it drops into the muffler. The heat will explode the butane lighter, he claims.

Perhaps it would be well to test this on an abandoned car before it is really put to the test under field conditions. If this suggestion bothers more sensitive readers, then simply turn the premise to the negative, i.e., don't shove butane lighters into automobile mufflers.

Camping

One of Canada's prime tricksters is also a camping aficionado. But, as Ron Lank likes his privacy and peace undisturbed, he sometimes runs into unruly campers who don't follow this golden rule of the wilds. Ron has developed some ways for dealing with crude and rude campers.

Ron says that empty bug repellent bottles can be washed out thoroughly and then be refilled with something sweet like pancake syrup or sugar water . . . sure to draw insects. The bogus juice is then left in the mark's campsite where it will be used.

"This stuff works well at night when the drunks just see the label and slap the stuff on. Sometimes, so many mosquitos show up the poor mark is tempted to give up camping forever. But no such luck, the bad ones seldom do," Ron reports.

Another Lank trick is to get into conversation with the rude campers, then bring up the "snake problem" at that campsite. Tell the mark that the snakes aren't really a problem because they come out only at night when everyone is inside his camper or tent, all zipped up and snakeproof.

"Besides, I don't believe that rumor about three people being bitten by snakes this past week. At least nobody died, anyway!

"You might also ask the mark if he has a snakebite kit. Tell him he should maybe have two of them—just in case."

Ron once camped next to a group that had a loud, non-stop

party all night. The following day, while the revelers slept, Ron scouted up a nearby poison ivy patch, then quietly swiped all the firewood from the drunkards' campsite. He put a few sticks in the poison ivy patch. When they started their party up again at dusk, the drunks saw Ron's nice camp fire. Drunkenly missing their own wood and thinking they had burned it all the night before, they asked "Good Neighbor Ron" where he got his wood. Remember that poison ivy patch, gentle reader?

That's exactly where Ron sent them to gather firewood, knowing they'd not see the noxious weed at night. Ron was up and gone the following morning so he missed their itchy agony. However, before leaving he noted with a grin that the poison ivy patch had been thoroughly trampled and much of it had been uprooted by hand and tossed around as the drunks tore through there looking for firewood. There are other suggestions.

If your mark is camping in bear country, be sure to rub ground beef all over the roof of his/her car at night. Mix in some honey, too. Big, hungry bears will climb up on the hood and roof of the vehicle to get at the goodies. Hopefully, they will dent it, cave it in, and, at the very least, scratch it badly. If you do the same thing to the Mark's tent or camper, the bears might ruin that. This could be dangerous, because the bruins might destroy the mark, also. But, nobody ever said camping was easy.

Another favorite on the bruin menu is sardine oil. It is the best lure for bears, according to my hunter friends. You simply spray the sardine oil or pour it over your mark's equipment or vehicle. I've always thought bears were really neat animals. Now I know they are.

Another camping funbit comes from Jacques Beel. Again, rowdy folks who don't know enough to observe the quiet hours became the marks after an evening of keeping decent folks awake. The four bad guys had a large tent with an attached floor. This structure was their environmental envelope, as things turned out.

About 6 A.M., just as the sun was peeking a sleepy eye open over the hills, a 4 x 4 Jeep coasted to a stop beside the offenders' tent. Quietly, a person got out and hooked a rope from the vehicle's trailer hitch on the eight guying grommets on the tent. A few seconds later the Jeep spun out, dragging the lumpy, noisy envelope through a rough meadow at the edge of the campground, through a stream, roaring into the mucky edge of the nearby lake, then doing a high speed turn while the passenger in the Jeep cut the towing rope at the apex of the turn. Guided by that great law of physics, the tentful of marks tumbled end over battered end into four feet of water. Beel's vehicle roared off . . . unknown and forgotten by any witnesses. According to Beel, the only tragic note was that nobody drowned.

The same payback stunt was reported by a reader of the first volume, who said the job ended abruptly when the tent ripped loose in the middle of a bumpy road curve being taken at high speed. The tent and its marks slammed into a small tree, then rolled en masse into a mammoth briar patch. We'll just credit that one to Uncle Remus.

Campus

It seems this kid named Curry was a sneaky sort. While other students did their own term papers, Curry used to buy his already written. Or, he would hire a good journalism major to ghostwrite him an "A" paper. A couple of his peers decided some creative revenge was in order.

They plagiarized a few semi-obscure essays from some dustcovered literature books in a seldom-used portion of the university library. They had these short essays and poems typed under Curry's name and submitted them to the campus literary magazine.

Hilariously, the literary magazine adviser never saw "Curry's" essays, while the student editors had never been exposed to the obscure originals and did not recognize the scam. Thus, the plagiarized pieces went into the magazine. Within minutes of the publication's appearance on campus, the adviser was besieged by calls from distraught English department faculty members who hadn't had so much excitement since some wag suggested they elect the the campus water fountain chairperson. Naturally, in the time honored academic tradition, as the effluvia hit the fan, the mess filtered downward. The puzzled mark had to go through a campus hearing and until his influential parents brought pressure on the university, the kid's future there was bleak.

This scam may be used in another way, too. The same basic

plan will get a writer or reporter in trouble. Simply send plagiarized stuff in the mark's name to a professional publication. The stakes are much higher in this league, of course.

Candy

Every home or office has candy thieves . . . the folks who say, "Oh, I really shouldn't but . . . . " The worst ones, though, are those silent sneakers who empty your candy box while your back is turned. Here is a little appetizer for them. Collect dead insects from dusty window sills. Cover the little corpses with chocolate and put them in with the real candy. Bon appetit.

This one may take some getting used to, and you may not even want to read it . . . it's pretty yukky. But, it came in and is sworn to as true by the perpetrator. It shows me how far people will go when they are frustrated or screwed over by someone else. Our source here is a man who wants to call himself The Phantom from Whitman's Samplers. You'll see the cogency in a moment.

Mr. Phantom got fired without cause by his very rotten boss, but only after the young employee had set up a system of accounting which would save the company a lot of money. After the employee set up the system and explained it, the boss fired him and turned it over to his wife to operate. Wives don't have to be paid, I guess.

Mr. Phantom's revenge was, ahh, sweet. Here's his story.

"My ex-boss was having a party for some of his equally crass friends. I decided to send along a present of my own 'homemade candy' which I had an ally, a friendly bartender, slip into the party.

I made sure my present was all done up nicely in a Whitman Sampler box with real candy. Here's how I prepared that gift.

"Several nights before the party I ate six ears of corn for dinner . . . nothing else. Later that evening, I ate two apples (a great source of pectin). The next morning I moved my bowels into a plastic bag. I allowed the feces to dry in the sun for two days. Wearing rubber gloves, I cut that dried block into small squares the size of cherries. They were semihard with whole kernels of corn running through them, a decidedly disgusting visual effect.

"Then, I melted four large bars of milk chocolate in a double boiler, and, not unlike a fondue, I gently covered the feces pieces with the delectable milk chocolate.

"When they were dry, I wrapped each one in the golden foil that the original chocolate-covered cherries come wrapped in. I filled the box and resealed it."

According to Mr. Phantom, the bartender said the "gift" was devoured for a few moments until one guest finally spit out a piece of "candy." Within two minutes, there was not enough bathroom space to accommodate eighteen gastrically ill guests involuntarily intent upon regurgitating.

Carbide

Having been brought up around hunters and miners, I learned all about carbide lamps and carbide fishing early. Working on my grandfather's farm, I learned about carbide bombs. Let me explain some things you might find useful.

When calcium carbide is exposed to air and water it produces a gas that will kill small animals. Farmers often pour it down gopher, rat, or groundhog holes, then dump in some water and put a rock over the hole. The animal is gassed to death.

A lot of poor people used to fish with carbide with the same efficiency with which legions of GIs fished with hand grenades. Simply toss a pound or two of carbide into a can and seal it, but be sure to punch a few holes in the lid. Toss it into a pond. The results can play havoc with your mark's fish pond or fancy goldfish pool or an indoor aquarium. Water and carbide can produce an explosion.

Some of the nastier kids used to place amounts of carbide into the toilets at our school. The idea was to place the carbide bomb in the toilet, leave a lighted cigarette on the seat, and run like hell. The carbide would combine with the water to produce a huge cloud of noxious gas, which would explode when it hit the lighted cigarette the perpetrators left behind. This little homemade bomb did more damage than an M80.

Tim Bell, who later became a Special Forces NCO in Vietnam, explains, "We had this kid bully whom no one liked—a real prick. He always went to the john after fourth period to sneak a smoke. So two of us went in right after him and laid a carbide bomb in the water in the next stall. We were about a hundred feet down the hall when the damn thing went off."

At this point, Tim burst into wild laughter. I was able to learn, though, that the bully had his legs burned and cut by flying porcelain, bit his tongue badly, was knocked violently off the throne, bruising his ribs against the steel wall of the stall, and was deafened for nearly twenty-four hours, all by the force of this carbide explosion. With that kind of background as a high school kid, it's no wonder Tim Bell made a good Special Forces trooper.

Are there more adult uses for carbide? Some sixties semi-terrorists used to dump a pound or so into the toilets of corporate offices and government buildings, flush the mess into the system, and walk away briskly. Enough of the stuff could get very dangerous, considering the possible backup of gases. A combination of water and carbide has been fed into the ventilating systems of various corporate and government buildings, also by semiterrorists who wish to harass the resident bureaucrats.

Careers

Your mark might be a college senior or might just be someone else who needs a job reference. A friend of mine used to be a college instructor, until he finally got bored with the genetic drift being admitted as undergraduates to America's campuses these days, and went back to his former occupation as a corporate personnel manager. But, his idea is a real tribute to unequal opportunity employment.

"I found out these two students had been forging my signature to all sorts of official college documents—grade change forms, class schedules, academic excuses, etc. They were advisees of mine and I felt they were violating a great academic trust and damaging that fragile student-professor relationship, not to mention the fact that the sneaky little bastards just plain pissed me off.

"A visit to the campus job placement office brought me two blank reference letter forms, and my devious sense of creative vindictiveness did the rest," he explained.

What our avenging academic did was complete a total ficticious recommendation for each offending student. He created a bogus professorial name and title, then wrote two masterfully done reference letters that absolutely sliced each student into tiny slivers. For instance, he wrote of one, "Although he may seem indolent, perhaps this is just his way of cautiously studying the situation." Or, consider this career bon mot, " ———

exhibited that good old Yankee spirit of free enterprise by offering to write term papers for his fellow student in return for money." He also wrote, "Showing knowledge outside the classroom _____ tells me he feels the real word can be found in the barrooms, poolhalls and other social power centers within the community." My friend brought both politics and religion to his marks' reference letters, writing, "It takes guts these days to be a public advocate of atheism (student #1) Marxism (student #2), and _____ stands up boldly and loudly for what he believes in."

Our former professor says he signed the bogus reference letters and sent them to the job placement office. The clerk there duly logged them, and they were placed with the students' credentials.

"I know it worked because I had a businessman friend of mine request a copy of each student's file. My nasty reference letters were in there. My friend who got the copies for me was aghast that the 'students had been so stupid to have someone with such a poor opinion of them write a letter of recommendation.' I just smiled at that. My friend didn't know about my scam. It proved my point."

Cemeteries

Once when the father of a friend of mine died, the family lawyer—supposedly a trusted "friend" of the deceased—turned out to be a real sphincter muscle, screwing up the widow's benefits, inheritence, and losing the deceased's retirement money in redtape.

Shortly after the financial disaster, my friend began to badger the telephone company and the local cemetary in the name of the lawyer, making all sorts of wild requests for a special telephone hookup for his casket. Posing as the mark, my friend explained he had this fear of being buried alive. He kept this up for months.

Finally, the lawyer convinced the people at the telephone company and the cemetery that he was the victim of a hoax. He also sought police protection because he feared some psycho was out to kill him—the hints about caskets, death, etc. In final desperation, he called my friend and almost begged him to tell the truth—was he behind the terror tactics? My friend says he just laughed his most chilling J.R. Ewing laugh into the phone and hung up. Later that afternoon, he mailed the lawyer a "Sympathy on the death in your family" card. He did this off and on for another month.

He then went to an anti-establishment tabloid newspaper and paid them to run the lawyer's obituary as an advertisement. They were happy to do it, needing both the money and a good laugh at the discomfort of the badgered barrister. Seeing the notice, the editor of the local daily quickly called the lawyer's family "to see if all was well?" When the harried mark took his family on a sudden vacation within that week, my friend then ran an ad "in his behalf" in the local daily. The ad said the mark's law firm would be closed for several days because of a death in the family.

My friend quit when a friend of his, a local police investigator who was no friend of the attorney either, told him he was close to getting in trouble. My friend took the hint . . . for the time being.

Chemicals

Dr. Doyle Conan, our medical adviser, said to mention gentian violet as a great helper. Officially, it is a powdered substance used for washing laboratory slides. But a problematic side effect is that it stains the skin a rich shade of deep purple and is nearly impossible to wash off. According to Dr. Conan, it takes a week of repeated scrubbing to remove the stain.

"The stuff is nontoxic, so you can put it in a spraying device to annoint offending animals, children, ex-lovers, etc.," Dr. Conan claims.

Conjuring up an old experience from the Hayduke Depository of Rotten Things I've Done to Deserving Folks, a friend and I had gotten some gentian violet one summer and sprinkled the powder on some snooty bitches as they lay sunning their vain bodies around a country club swimming pool. A combination of perspiration, oil, and heat caused the powder to stick. As the light staining began, the young ladies raced to the pool to wash off the offending and spreading color. I leave the rest to your imagination.

You remember the book *Black, Like Me?* Credit silver nitrate, also known as lunar caustic, for the ability to blacken one's skin. According to the Rev. J. Richard Young, one ounce of this in a standard bottle of suntan oil will cause the mark's afflicted parts to turn quite black for several days. It is also highly soluble in warm water, which can be sprayed.

I once knew a hospital orderly in the service who used it on a truly racist soldier whose waking moments were spent cursing blacks. The orderly gave the bigot a sponge bath with a solution containing a good dose of silver nitrate. In a day the man's color went from Redneck to Ethnic Dark. A nurse in on the gag told him that his last blood transfusion had been donated by a soldier of the Negro persuasion. It never changed the bigot's mentality, but it surely blew his mind for a few days.

Another reader who used silver nitrate was Marie from New Orleans, who said she mixed it into some shaving cream owned by a friend who had done her an injustice. It worked just fine, as she reports with a chuckle about his unwanted man tan.

A nasty chemical known as copper sulfate is deadly poisonous to aquatic life, as any sportsman knows. Farmers know it is also very injurious to trees. If, for some ungodly reason, you want to kill someone's aquatic life or trees, this stuff will do the trick. Two pounds dumped into a pond will do the job, while four ounces poured around the drip line—the outer edge of the leaves of any given tree—will murder the tree. Personally, I'd rather hurt people than fish or trees.

The canny Rev. J. Richard Young offers a fantastic tear gas substitute for nasty dogs, cats, rats, bats, kids, and for use during domestic spats. Go to a chemical supply house and buy Formaldehyde 97%. Tell them you or your kid has a big insect collection or something. Put it in a nasal spray bottle and fire away. It will temporarily knock the socks off anything hit in the face with it.

It's no lie, says Herb Bobwander, that lye is a great tool for the trickster. Herb suggests you wrap some lye in a newspaper, fasten it with rubber bands, then drop or throw this projectile onto your mark's car roof, roof gutters, or other areas you want to be eaten through. The lye will ruin paint, eat holes in soft metals, plus stain paint, and kill vegetation. Now that's what I call the right stuff.

Christmas Trees

Stoney Dale used to live two doors away from a cantankerous old man who never had a kind word for anyone. The man verbally abused his neighbors and their kids and pets, took potshots with a BB gun, or was always calling the police for things he imagined people were doing to him. The police regarded him as a crank and dreaded his calls. Stoney took it upon himself to get even on behalf of the suffering neighborhood.

"Two days past Christmas I ran an ad in the local paper, saying, 'I have a need for all evergreen trees used for Christmas decoration. Please leave them on my driveway or lawn. I will pay you $3 per tree.' I used the old grump's name and address with the ad. The newspaper took my cash and never checked the story. Within two days the old man's property was buried with the remains of the town's Yuletide," Stoney relates.

Classified Ads

All good Americans are born bargain hunters, expecially when the price is free. But, I had this acquaintance who was beyond amazingly cheap. I have actually seen him scarf up tips from other people's tables at restaurants. He had to be paid back, as it were.

One day I placed an ad in his local newspaper saying that my mark had free cocker spaniel puppies to give away. The following week I did it with kittens. I let him go a week, then I had him giving away manure. Next, he was selling used guns that I priced about 20 percent below the normal price. I made the rounds of the local shops that allow people to post personal want ads on index cards. I started him all over again in this medium. In each message I included his telephone number and told people to call well after midnight because of shift work.

The final phase involved those classified personals in sleazy sex publications. This worked well because this cheap mark and his wife were ultra straight, born-again religious freaks whose attitudes about fun stuff was expressed in terms of "if God had wanted us to be naked, He would have had us born that way." When he began to get really kinky responses to the really kinky ads I placed in his name, the tolerance and Christian patience of his equally boring wife was stretched beyond turning her other well-padded cheek. Last I heard they were attending additional crash courses in dissolving lustful thoughts, or going cold turkey on even thinking about procreation. But, he hasn't been out in public since then to pick up someone else's tips.

College Life

Jim Klann has a check-bouncing idea that he used to pull on slobs and others who did rotten things to him while he was working his way through college. It was relatively simple, and it will work on almost any mark, not just college students, in lots of situations.

"I would place a call to the mark, identify myself as the college bursar and inform him that his last tuition check had just bounced. If it was his check, that was it. If it was his parents' check, I told him to call home immediately.

"I always called about three minutes before five o'clock so that if he asked for more details like the amount or check number, I could mumble something about the file clerk already locking up the records and that the office was closing. Then, I'd get stern again and tell him to call us back first thing in the morning."

Jim's scam had the mark calling home and worrying all night about bouncing a check, owing service fees, and good stuff like that.

Irritated because some mature and outstanding young men who belonged to the right social fraternity at the University of Illinois stole, molested, and terrorized his date, then threw up on his car, a fellow student who was majoring in Haydukery came up a winner. There was an outdoor beer party at the fraternity that afternoon. Our man had another student walk over and tell the frat guys that some students from another campus were going to try to crash the party that afternoon, only they'd be dressed as local cops. Then, later, our hero called the local cops to complain about the lawn party.

Later, this same student was awakened one morning by a crew of surly construction workers from another town. They were busily and noisily digging up the sidewalk in front of his room. It was 6:08. He dressed and went to his eight o'clock class early. On his way out, he stopped and talked with a couple of the workers. He told them that the last time a crew worked near campus, a bunch of fraternity guys dressed up as campus cops tried to hassle the workers as a practical joke. The workers didn't like this idea one bit.

Later, just before going into his class, our agitator called the campus police office and told them a bunch of fraternity guys were dressed up as a construction crew and were digging up the sidewalk at such and such an address. When they asked him who he was, he gave them the name of the president of the fraternity mentioned earlier.

Aren't you sorry you didn't go to school with Joe from New Orleans? He's the guy who epoxy'd shut a deserving mark's dorm room door the night before the kid's most important final exams. Why did Joe do this?

"He (the mark) was a badass, always coming in drunk and blowing his dinner on us, after a beer party; you know, throwing up in our rooms. Nothing nice to correct him worked, so we figured if we made him miss his finals, he'd flunk the courses and be out of school."

In another case, one of Joe's dormmates from another floor used to think it was great fun to turn in false fire alarms. That costs everyone something and is a stupid thing to do. Joe didn't think it was too funny either. He got several surplus fire extinguishers on the sly from a sympathetic fireman friend, and they filled the mark-who-cried-fire's room with foam while the kid lay in a drunken stupor.

If you thought Joe was nasty, try Kevin from the same grand old city over there in Louisiana. His mark was a bully who was always doing nasty things to nice people. Kevin gave him a double-barreled dose of his own meanness. He waited until the mark boldly announced he was going to cut a few days of classes to go shack up with some campus tootsie he'd picked up in a bar. Kevin then called the school administration and each of the mark's teachers and told them that he (Kevin) was the undertaker (using a real name) from the mark's hometown and that the kid had died suddenly and to please take him off the class lists, enrollment files, and the master computer list. He said a letter and death certificate would follow by mail. Then, Kevin's buddy posed as a school official, called the mark's parents and told them their son was dead as a result of a party prank. Kevin never went near the mark again. A lot of other people did though, and the mark had a lot of explaining to do.

Wouldn't it be neat to get a bunch of course withdrawal forms from some office on campus and fill them out in your mark's name? You could then feed them to the computer through the appropriate clerk and have the mark officially withdrawn from classes. The poor mark, of course, will continue to go to class, take tests, do assignments, worry about grades, and all that good stuff. Only at the end of the term will he or she realize what happened.

Condoms

Big Jules Torquato of Newark came up with a piercing twist to the old idea of sticking holes in condoms. It seems his sister was living with her supposedly faithful sweetheart. Then, one day little sister found a hefty supply of Trojans. She thought this a bit odd since she was on the pill. Then she recalled the late nights, the early mornings, the excuses, the odd odors, and other things about her lover's behavior of late that didn't add up—until she found the hidden condoms.

Jules' sister put the venerable pin pricks in the rubber goods, then put them back carefully so that Mr. Wrong would continue to rely on their effectiveness. When Jules found out about all of this, he added the final touch (ouch!). He carefully skewered a large pin into the last condom, as a signal that its owner had misplaced his trust in his organ as much as Jules' little sister had in him.

Contractors

Just suppose your new home wasn't what the contractor ordered and promised. If you're lucky, you'll discover this fact before he's done working on the house. If not, you'll have to chase him to his next job site. I once went through that many years ago, and it can be fun.

Here's what you do. Erect a huge sign on your lot that says something like, BUY THIS UNDER-CONSTRUCTED, POORLY DONE HOME—CHEAP. Display the contractor's name and telephone number prominently. When he complains, tell him you wouldn't think of subjecting your family to the horrors of living in such a poorly constructed dump, and if he buys it you'll take down the sign. Have a list of things you think are wrong with the house. You have already shown him your list if you had to eventually resort to the big sign. Show him again. The heading of the list should state his name, address, and telephone number along with your general beef about the poor quality of his work, followed by the specific complaints. Make copies of this list so your contractor will think you're handing them out left and right. You should get your grievances satisfied.

A man calling himself Hank suggested one for the construction trade. He says that if your mark is building anything from concrete and you or your allies have access to that concrete before it is poured, add concentrated hydrochloric acid to it. Hank claims, "I've seen it work—it causes slow but continual deterioration of the structure from corrosion."

Convenience Stores

If you'd like to add a secondary mark to your revenge on a guilty convenience store, enjoy this idea sent along by Sam Stein, a Connecticut Hayduker with a great sense of humor. Sam says to call the store and have them set aside about ten copies of today's newspaper and hold them for _____ (secondary mark's name). If the papers arrive at 2:00 P.M., call about 3:30, as this will give them time to sell most copies and be down to the last ones for rush-hour traffic commuters. In any case, when you gather your intelligence, note numbers of papers and times sold so you are sure to reserve the last copies.

You tell the clerk that you'll pick up your copies within the hour as you're coming from work. By 5:30, the salesclerk usually calls the mark's home. If he or she is home, the clerk may complain, but, usually, they'll get things straightened out. If the mark's not home, it works even better.

Call the clerk back about 6:30 and say you were delayed in traffic and are still intending to pick up the newspapers. Tell the clerk you'll be there by 7:00. The clerk will probably raise hell. Try innocence. Blame "your brother" for answering your phone at home, playing a joke on him/her, and of course you want the papers. Be adamant.

Call the store at 7:30 and tell the clerk you don't want the papers anymore because the news is all old. The clerk will really raise hell now. You should get abusive. Repeat who is calling. Use the mark's name often and threaten the clerk.

Other things you can tell the clerk are that you'll trash the store, burn it down, burn his or her car, or torture him/her. If the clerk threatens to call the police, tell him to go ahead and try. Say you'll be down there in three minutes to kill him *and* the "gawdamn pig-cops."

Within moments, the police will be rushing Code 3 to your mark's home in swarms with all lights and sirens blaring. Sam says that if the cops don't show because the clerk failed to call, then visit the store that night and toss a brick through the window or dump the mark's garbage in the store or on the sidewalk (see *Garbage*). Then, start the entire process over again.

Conventions

Although billed under the Conventions heading, these monkey warfare ideas will work well at any conference, meeting or semi-serious gathering. They could also be used for some of those combination business/social functions that our corporate cancers love so much. The first suggestion came from the fertile mind of Col. Friedkin Maximov, propaganda officer of the Student Liberation Army, an anarchist group of folks whose motto is "All power to the trash heap."

They pulled this gemlet off during the 1978 National Student Association and National Student Lobby conventions. Their first step was intelligence gathering about who the key officials were, where they were staying and where and when the key meetings would be held. Next, a supply of forged credentials and memoranda were gathered. Most of the memoranda were from one official to another and covered such topics as moving key meeting times and places; moving banquets ahead an hour; denying rumors of an outbreak of Legionnairé's Disease; bomb threat denials; and a preliminary evacuation plan, "just in case." Dated and timed for appropriate dissemination, the memos created chaos and spread confusion and mistrust throughout the convention. Col. Maximov says it took several hours to get things under semi-control, but the bug of paranoia had been sown.

You really don't have to be Abbie Hoffman or even Philo Freed to sabotage a convention. According to Jim Brownie, here's all you do.

"You know the current vogue is to have circus type clowns at conventions . . . decorated, and all that. There are 'Rent-A-Clown' places in most all major cities. Why not hire your own clowns?

"You get your own special pranksters, who will 'work' in addition to the real clowns. The idea is to dress yours the same way. Of course, while the establishment-convention clowns are doing gentle, good natured stuff, your clowns are spilling peoples' drinks on other people, honking stuffy society matrons' boobs, pinching asses, spitting on important people, exposing themselves, handing out dirty pictures, etc."

He adds that shortly pandemonium will result, by which time you and your clowns are gone. The convention planners will garner the blame for this one, regardless of their shameless denials.

I have this friend who is a minor league Ted Turner, in that while Turner enjoys expensive wine, women, song and athletic competition, my pal digs booze, broads, boogie and sports. He told me how he once got chewed out by the executive director of his professional association, a very stuffy sort—I know the man, too—for coming drunk to a convention dinner and burping a few times. He also nuzzled his wife openly. I mean, what the hell, he didn't pinch her banquet buns or anything. Anyway, he caught hell from this pious old poop. A seed of revenge hatched that very evening. My friend took six months to set up his scam. He waited until the association's Fall meeting.

"I hired a very attractive and uninhibited couple, a call girl and a sex film performer, to attend the association dinner. I purchased guest tickets for them in the name of the executive director. She wore a gown right off the rack at Frederick's of Hollywood. She looked great. So did the stud she came with. They attracted a lot of attention just in looks.

"As the executive director started his usual, boring 30-minute

71

pre-dinner monotone, my ringers started to nuzzle each other. Within moments, attention left the podium and was zeroed in on my hired couple. They were panting away, kissing with their tongues tied around each others. Then, the guy's hand pops into the loose gown and out comes a breast to be played with. You can guess where his other hand goes next. She's groaning and tugging at this pants, moaning about how much she wants to 'voluntarily perform an unnatural sex act' (that sort of wording keeps my editor happy) on him.

"I'm not joking, before anyone could make a move, his pants are off and he hoists her right up on the table and they start going at it. No lie, it was great, they were really going at it. My wife and I started to applaud. So did a few other young couples. Our association director almost had a stroke. His wife (they deserve each other) fainted. Anyway he killed the lights in the hall, which of course, just added to the confusion.

"I was high on humor and started to throw food. So did the folks. Without going into more detail, let me assure you the rest of the convention died at that point. It was the funniest thing I have ever seen and the greatest thing I have ever done in the name of personal freedom. The executive director has never lived that one down . . . even today, six years later."

Corporations

Although this scam will work best with large corporations, you could adapt it to smaller companies or organizations as well. Obviously, by this far into our dirty tricks alphabet, you must know that you should have just cause for your revenge!

After your basic intelligence gathering and planning stage, you need to acquire an original and official letterhead and envelope from the mark. One way to obtain that letterhead/envelope is to innocently write the company for information. Or, visit the offices and swipe some during a lunch hour or just at quitting time. A good Xerox-type machine and some skills explained in Volume I will give you your own supply of "official" letterheads. Or, your friendly printer could do the same thing.

Next, using that new letterhead, write a sharply worded business letter from Company A to Company B, demanding payment for merchandise, equipment, etc. Then, using Company B's "official" letterhead, write Company A a nasty letter complaining of faulty merchandise, equipment, etc., and threatening personal injury damages from same.

In your research and intelligence phase you need to obtain the names and, if possible, the signatures of some middle managers who will "sign" your letters. Now, you mail them and await the communication fun.

Dead Bodies

Sorry, I didn't know what else to call this one, as it really doesn't involve human cadavers. But, let Abe Mirthal explain—it was his idea in the first place.

"When I went to Virginia Beach and other Atlantic coastal resorts I used to see an oceanic novelty in the various souvenir shops. It was something known as a sea-monkey or devilfish. The novelty was the dried up skin of this creature. It looked strikingly like a tiny, shriveled up human body."

Abe suggests that you may know someone who would be horrified to see or receive one of these creatures dressed in soiled doll clothing or some other format/scenario that might be appropriate. As always, think of some way to make your punishment fit the mark's crime against you. Perhaps you can use Abe's creatures to get even some way.

The only time he personally knew of this being used was to terrorize a child molester who had hired an oily attorny to get him out of the charges. Both the molester and his accomplice, the legal hitman, got several exposures to these horrid visions. Word is the molester soon moved to another city and the attorney limited himself to corporate practice—which hardly seems like contrition to me!

Delicatessens

The only bad thing about The Clay Demolay Delicatessen is the fact that bugs, insects, and other many-legged vermin are among its best customers. While the employees begged for sanitation improvements, the owner, Myers Demolay, just chortled and counted his profits. One of these employees, whom we'll call Deliboy Dave, finally tired of begging for better working conditions. He decided to bug the boss, literally.

"One summer, we had a mammoth order for hoagies that I had to prepare. The big horse flies were buzzing all around as I worked," Deliboy Dave recounts, "so, I started using two pieces of provolone cheese as a compression fly swatter. I'd blast a few bugs between the two slices of cheese, leaving the small corpses and attendant gore on the slices.

"Then, I'd add the fly 'n' guts garnished slices to the hoagies on our assembly line. Nobody noticed, and about one hundred-fifty hoagies went out that day. I didn't work the next day, but I was told that some eighty irate people stormed the place."

Delivery of Consumables

For years kids have ripped off beer distributors' trucks, pizza wagons, etc. The scam is to call the place from a pay phone and give them a fake name in some high-rise apartment. Give them the pay-phone number and stick around there for a while, since some places call back to confirm orders. When the truck arrives with the order, and while he is up there trying to find a nonexistent customer, you could help yourself to what's left in the truck.

Why would anyone rip off an innocent beer-delivery truck or pizza wagon? Fred Littman has one reason, saying, "I ordered a pizza at one place locally, and it was awful. I spoke with the manager, and he told me to get lost and refused to give me my money back. I figured I had some free pizza coming to make up for that."

Lefty Gaylor has another reason: "We swipe beer from only one distributor, because everyone knows he's a big Mafia type, and they rip off everyone else, so why not steal from them?"

Isn't stealing from the Mafia dangerous?

"Not if you don't get caught, and this one's too dumb to know any better. He blames the drivers, and they get mad and figure if they're gonna get blamed, they might as well steal beer from him. That way we multiply our efforts."

Perhaps the Justice Department could find some use for Lefty and his boys.

Dirty Old Men

If you know some jerk who's a terminal lecher, not just a dirty old man, but a truly, grossly obnoxious swine, the following is a sure-fire method that's right on target. You need either three or four associates, depending on whether you personally want to go into the field on this one. One of your associates must be comely young lady.

The drill goes like this. The mark is told about the young lady. She is described as being either an unfaithful wife or a hot-to-trot daughter, depending on the age and circumstance. The mark is told she has eyes and everything else for him, and that if he wants to have a lot of heavy action, you or an associate will make the introduction.

As you approach the fateful house on the evening decided upon, you or your associate, acting as "guide," must stress that the husband or father is a fiery and jealous man and that she takes you on as a secret lover because of insatiable lust, etc. Build up both the sexual suspense and the thrill of the forbidden. You have to get his adrenaline and imagination cooking really well.

The mark and his guide are at the door and the sweet young thing opens it and moans out a greeting. She should be dressed—or undressed—in an appropriate fashion. The mark should have just enough time to wet his lips and survey her architectural lines. About the time his eyes bug is time for the next act.

Instantly, a large man comes roaring around the corner of the house, bellowing in rage about the honor of his wife or daughter. The guide screams in shrill terror, "Run! Run like hell! It's the husband [or father] !"

As the mark and guide start to dash away, a couple of shots are fired, and the guide falls. As he falls, he screams to the mark, "Jesus, keep running! He's killed me!" Another shot rings out; then all is silent.

All is not really silent. The mark's heart is probably thudding against his chest like a caged elephant. It's a great idea to carry on with this scenario for a few days, with you or another conspirator, who has been undercover, keeping the mark apprised of the guide's condition from the supposed gunshot wound. It would also be good to float the rumor that the father or husband is spending all his time looking for "the other bastard who got away."

The mark won't stop his fearful shakes long enough to wonder why the police haven't arrested the husband or father. Maybe, when he does come to this logical question, he will call the police and ask for protection. This scam turns a lot of corners before the mark finally realizes that he's been had. The police probably won't be as amused as you are, but you'll not know about that. The mark will.

If you know the right street people, and if you're going into dirty tricks you must know them, you will have trickster access to ladies with social diseases. Some of the veterans of the streets will help you out between treatments for a price. Younger, less-experienced ladies don't know they have the diseases, but their pimp or madam does. Think how much fun it would be if you could hire one of these venereal versions of Typhoid Mary to dazzle, pick up, and seduce your mark. This scam has been pulled off successfully by at least four people I know personally. It is not that hard if you plan, bargain, and buy ahead.

Drugs

Two readers of my initial literary effort wrote to tell me that Yohimbine really is a medical aphrodisiac. One, a pharmacist, says it really will work. It is used by veterinarians and if handled carefully would be both safe and effective with humans. The key word he stressed was safety. I wonder if that is before or after the inclusion of the drug? The other reader claimed to be a "field tester." He didn't say of what. In any case, his terse message was, "Yohimbine is the real thing. It can really buzz up a chick."

Contributor Ellen James writes that her idea is more of a practical joke than a dirty trick. But, it's nothing to snort at because it's sure to tweak the noses of some marks. In any case, the scene is one of those posh cocaine settings where everyone is "oh so ready to do a few lines." You gently smuggle a bit of milk sugar in your place in line, as it were. When it's your turn to pull 'er in . . . you suddenly choke, puff, then sneeze like fury . . . blowing the milk sugar all over the atmosphere. The heads think you've just wasted umpteen dozen dollars worth of coke. And, well, as she said, it's more of a joke. The ending's up to you.

Fifteen U.S. Air Force officers and enlisted men assigned to operate a nuclear missile silo in Arizona were suspended from duty after two joints of potent marijuana were discovered by security guards on the control room floor. Think of the possibilities for sabotage. Think of the possibilities for planting evidence to incriminate your mark.

Another reader passed along the nature lore that Hawaiian Baby Woodrose seeds, *Argyreia nervosa,* are a potent hallucinogen. He also claims that common Morning Glories can be distilled into a homemade LSD-like concoction. Have a good trip, because some other folks are on a bad journey now.

Malcolm Miller was simply a middle class pissant, until he turned in some friends who were making private and moderate use of *cannabis sativa* among themselves. After paying a moderate fine and getting suspended sentences from some drunken hypocrite of a Nixonian judge, our heroes decided to get back at their pot pooper.

They obtained some medicine bottles of the type in which prescriptions are dispensed. One of them lifted a pad of prescription labels from a small pharmacy. They typed labels in the name of the mark, then included the instruction, "Take one every four hours for penis infection." They also typed labels for him, "infecting" him with pinworms, VD, trenchmouth, alcoholism, opiate reaction, herpes, etc. The bottles began to appear around his area at work, in his car, in his wife's car, etc.

Electrical

If this bit hadn't come from former CIA man Miles Kendig I would put it down as a shocking parlor trick that will short out your mark's lights.

Here's how it works. Select a *wall switch operated* electrical appliance that will conduct the trick for your mark, such as a table lamp, TV set, stereo, table top oven, etc. Make certain the power switch is in the OFF mode. Then, pull out the appliance's plug from the wall receptacle. Take a steel paperclip and place each end of the clip over the two prongs on the appliance's male plug. Slide the steel paperclip down to the base of the plug. Plug the appliance back in. Do NOT turn on the power mode switch; leave that for your mark. When he or she hits the power switch. . . . KABLOOOEY. . . a violently major short circuit takes place, and all sorts of things blow out. Miles says if you're lucky you might get a whole house outage from this trick.

Elevators

After the first book came out I did a lot of radio and TV interviews because many media people thought my concept of getting even was fairly amusing. Several of the interviewers got into the spirit of my creative revenge and suggested their own ideas for this second volume. Many of those are in this book. But, only a few of the media people would allow me to use names. So, here goes one of them.

David Hall of WQXI in Atlanta once had reason to be furious with the administrators of his college during undergraduate days. The beef had to do with visiting hours, curfews and a high-rise dormitory building. A non-engineer, Hall spent one hour rewiring the floor indicator buttons behind the electric panel behind the floor indicator buttons of the dorm's elevator.

Hall says, "I rewired buttons and stops so the floors and the indicators didn't match. For example, someone would punch the button for 5 and end up on 10. Or, they'd hit 8 and end up on 2, things like that. I did it on Saturday night when everyone was likely to come late and drunk. It was hilarious."

Even more hilarious was Hall's report that it took the university's electricians an entire day to get the machine coordinated again.

Employers

Want to get your tax money's worth out of an employer who's done you dirty? An earnest, "decent citizen doing his or her duty" telephone call to OSHA, the state health authorities, or the local fire inspector will get results in the form of a safety inspection. Even if the mark's place is clean, which is probably only a 50/50 shot from what I've seen while moving about the country, the bureaucratic harrassment will not be appreciated in the least. The paperwork for even the innocent is staggering and expensive. If you strike it lucky there will be an investigation and hearing.

Explosives

Now that the feds have outlawed fireworks, you'd better save all the M80s you can find. Extremely versatile devices, M80s are excellent propellants for other substances. For example, this stunt started out as a dorm prank at Clapper Packer University but soon escalated into more deadly sport, which went like this. Put some fresh feces, the looser the better, into a large Baggie. Gently break the glass on a large-wattage lightbulb, but do not disturb the filament. Even more gently attach the filament to the fuse of the M80. Screw the bulb carefully back into a ceiling socket. Finally, move the bag of feces up and around the light fixture. Be certain the fuse and filament do not touch the feces, but see that the M80 is into the substance. Tape the bag to the ceiling.

Naturally, all this presupposes you have access to the mark's room or to a room where the mark is likely to be the one who comes in and turns on the light. One cautionary note: Be sure the light switch is off when you screw in the bulb. If it's not, you have about four seconds to avoid getting nasty coverage from the M80's blast. Done correctly, this is a spectacular stunt. As the designer of this one, George Dierk adds, "You don't have to limit your spatter substance to feces. Paint, cheap perfume, acid, and CS gas all have their place."

Gunpowder has a lot of uses in addition to filling up a

portion of cartridges. If your mark has an outdoor barbecue, you could sprinkle a cup of old-fashioned black powder around the bottom of the grill. When the powder ignites it will do so with a huge, whooshy flash, accompanied by a great white cloud of smelly smoke. I would hate to imagine the multiple effects of such a pyrotechnical display on one of those fancy grills powdered by LP gas. Wow!

Don't let your imagination rest with the cookout grill. Remember fireplaces, wood stoves, ovens, etc. The experts suggest you use black powder rather than the more modern smokeless powders. Black powder really works!

If you can't get a regular smoke-bomb device, a smoke grenade, or something real from the military, make your own. According to Doctor Abraham Hoffman, the noted chemist, you combine four parts sugar to six parts saltpeter (potassium nitrate). You heat this mixture over a very low flame until it starts to blend into a plastic substance. When it begins to gel, remove it from the heat and allow it to cool. He suggests you stick a few wooden match heads into the mass while it's still pliable. You also add a fuse at this point. The smoke device is nonexplosive and nonflammable. But a pound of this mixture will produce enough thick smoke to cover a city block. Watch which way the wind blows.

John E. Warrenburger likes to mess up people's nervous systems. One of his favorite nonlethal tricks involving nonexplosives is a good bit of cardiac theater.

John says, "I bundle a few of those road flares—the ones in the red jackets—together and wrap them with black plastic tape. Connect this with some coiled wiring to a ticking alarm clock and place it so your mark will get the full visual and aural effect."

Applause, applause, John. Only God and the mark's launderer will know how dastardly the frightening effect of the bogus bomb is on the mark's nervous system.

Fan Club Freaks

Sometimes fan club freaks are obnoxious, even dangerous. A radio station personality was actually assaulted by an Elvis freak because he wouldn't keep playing her favorite selections.

"I got back at her by puking a colorfully spectacular cascade of vomit from pizza, wine, carrots, and candy into a plastic bag a week later. I tossed in a whole bunch of vitamin capsules and other pills, then mailed it to her at work, telling her that the National Elvis Fan Club was donating this package of 'Elvis's Last Supper' to her."

Long live the King!

Fast Food Stores

Here's a switch. Suppose you work at one of these gastronomic whorehouses and want to get back at some of the absolute idiot customers who make your life awful. There are lots of people who stop at fast food shops and demand the world and everything else in the most obnoxious way. Want to pay them back . . . while still smiling?

- Freddie from San Antonio works at (don't you wish you knew?) and says when someone urinates him off, he coughs up huge wet hawkers and blows them into their food before serving it.
- Allen, who works in Boston, cools off his temper from dealing with an awful customer by walking into the cooler and placing pieces of used toilet paper between ground beef patties of a franchise favorite.
- Sid used to do worse when a customer upset him without reason where he cooked. He would actually dab little flecks of feces on their patties after he had cooked them.
- At nationally recognized franchises that feature fries, you'll think about Larry, the cook. If he is irritated the night before, without fail, the next morning he will pee into every French fry bin.

Perhaps Bob Grain was on the mark's end of one of these employee stunts. Maybe that's why he drove to his local fast food outlet that used an outdoor two-way "drive-in" order device. Bob says he ordered a huge, expensive, and complicated meal, then immediately drove on through the line and away, far away.

I asked one of my moles inside a local fast food mark about this. She said there was a very good chance that the people in the car behind Bob's would get the order. If it were a big, complicated order, there would be an argument. If it were small, they might pay for it before realizing something was wrong. Hopefully, by then, as Bob noted, their kids would have it scattered all over the car. Of such wonders are dreams made? My mole says the best time to pull this off would be the busy times at lunch and during evening meal hours. She says it will work.

May I take your order?

Fears

Most people fear the unknown. Dr. Paul Wilson, a noted psychic, says, "That old fear of the dark, of the bogeyman, of what lies under our beds at night is with us all to some extent or another." George W. Hayduke, Jr., a noted rotten person, says this universal fear can be used to your advantage against almost any mark.

Odd noises at night, strange lights and/or sounds, bizarre telephone calls, cult and occult pictures sent through the mail, someone staring at the mark . . . all sorts of things can be done to prey on the mark's insecurities. Fear belongs; use it wisely.

Fish

I never knew how emotional people were about aquariums and tropical fish life until I heard a person at a party tearfully tell how the heater in his tank malfunctioned and turned that watery world into a large fish fry. Amazing.

If for some reason you want to get back at one of these fish fanatics, you could always slip a few Alka-Seltzer tablets in the tank. Or, if you were of a more terminal mind, try adding some small water snakes to that closed environment. You could also hook up a current activator or submersible heater to your mark's room light switch. That way, when he or she comes in and hits the light switch, they act as the executioner.

Flowers

Barbara from Chicago once lost her man to a true tramp. Using her mind rather than her body to fight back, Barbara sent this hussy a floral arrangement in the man's name. Included amid all the "ohh and ahh" pretty posies were selected portions of poison ivy.

Food

Labels come off food cans very easily, according to Margaret Dayton, kindly contributor to this volume. If you can get to the mark's food supply, switch and reglue some of the labels, e.g., Campbell's Beef Chunks and Alpo could switch labels. Margaret cautions though that your mark may be such a slob as to not notice the difference. But, I bet the mark's dog will.

Margaret adds this same stunt can be used to gain revenge against a supermarket which has done something to deserve retribution.

An ice cream cone will go well on any day. If your mark likes ice cream, here's an idea. Collect a live cockroach or two, and put them into the cone before you have the ice cream packed in. Imagine his or her surprise when half a roach is spotted sticking out of a fresh bit of the ice cream.

One of my good friends who also works for my publisher suggested this idea, and it's pretty darned funny, to me. Basically, what you're doing is getting back at a vegetarian who has done you dirty. Because these people are so dedicated to their antimeatism, this trick usually works well.

My friend advised, "You just slip some bits of pork into their veggie food. It works well in salad, stews and soups. But, save some evidence so you can prove it. It's wonderful, especially if they've just hogged out on a whole load of your doctored food and are really devout vegetarians."

He reported in one instance where he saw this done, the mark lost his entire dinner—on the spot.

Garage Sales

Ever have a garage sale? Ever been to one? They're incredible, and they seem to bring out the most in the worst people. Even I, a thick-skinned, terminal misanthrope, was awed at the gall of some people who demand to see your entire house or who pound on your door at 6:00 A.M. to get a "head start" on a garage sale you announced in the paper as starting at 9:00 A.M. Getting the message?

Let's have a garage sale at your mark's residence. Or let's have it in your mark's name but at the neighbor's address. List all sorts of outlandish bargains and tell people you have guns, old china, glassware, and dozens of inexpensive antiques. You want obnoxious gawkers, not buyers. Remember that! Naturally, the mark and/or the neighbor will know nothing of this until the first knock on the door at 6:00 A.M.

"I used to get all sorts of odd-hour calls from home-remodeling and -repair salespeople at this one local company," recalls Jim Kenslogger. "I must have called them a half dozen times to ask that my name and number be removed from their files. No luck. So I decided to change my luck.

"I learned who their chief executive was and pulled the bogus-garage-sale number on him, complete with newspaper ad. Then I started calling his home at odd hours, asking if he were the party having the garage sale. He was really out of sorts after about a week of this.

"I stopped, and about ten days later I got another routine sales call from his company. I called right back, asked to speak to that executive, and told him I was damn tired of being bothered by his salespeople and could he get them to stop calling me. He pledged he would and told me wearily, 'Buddy, I know just how you feel. I'll surely take care of it for you.' I had no trouble after that, so neither did he."

Garbage

If my mail is any indicator, A.J. Weberman is not the only noted American garbologist. For example, The Night Lurker robs his mark's mailbox, removes only the junk mail, mixes it with various items of trash and garbage, then tosses them onto other people's lawns.

We can thank Stoney Dale for dragging out this tidbit of garbage. He had yet another grouchy neighbor who was hated by one and all. The man left for work at seven in the morning, while Stoney departed several hours later. In the meantime, the garbage truck made its rounds of the neighborhood. Stoney had a friend from another part of town stop by his house on garbage day, and here's what happened.

"Just as the garbage men pulled up in front of the Grinch's house, my friend would stroll down the mark's driveway like he lived there. He told the men that his wife had misplaced her watch and he was going to search the garbage for it. He told them not to worry about pickup," Stoney relates. "They didn't and soon left."

Stoney says the Grinch didn't say anything about his garbage bags being the only ones in evidence in the neighborhood that night. But when the following week rolled around, Grinch put out another set of bags. Stoney's pal pulled the same stunt. This time, when he got home from work, Grinch hit the ceiling. He asked Stoney what was going on, and Stoney played dumb. Grinch called the garbage people and raised hell with the dispatcher, who raised hell back. Result—it took two more weeks for Grinch to get another garbage removal company to come to his home and at a premium price. In the meantime, dogs had ripped open the huge pile of bags and crap was scattered all over the neighborhood. Stoney had another friend report Grinch to the police for littering. See the section on *Neighbors,* and if you live near Stoney Dale, be a good, friendly neighbor!

Gasoline

In his excellent book *They Were Expendable,* W. L. White writes about the first few months of WWII as it affected the men of a motor torpedo boat squadron. One segment of the book described a Japanese agent who sabotaged the American PT boats by pouring dissolved candle wax into their gasoline drums. Running this mixture through the engines created all sorts of nasty hell with filters, critical tolerances, etc. You don't have to be of the Japanese persuasion or even at war to adapt this gimmick to your mark's gasoline supply or even to his automobile, boat, tractor, snowmobile, or whatever. It would work in a gasoline powered generator, too, and in just about any engine powered by a petroleum fuel. That should brighten the light of your creative candle and allow you to wax eloquently upon this new use of this old dirty trick. Banzai!

Gates

Always open gates and leave them open when you're dealing with a mark who has a gate. There are lots of fringe benefits to this. For example, his expensive purebred dog might get out and run away. Or, someone or something terrifying could come in. Another benefit of vengeful gatekeeping is that you don't even have to trespass. Just opening the gate is enough.

When I was a kid, we had a mean old man in the neighborhood. He lived on an estate sitting in the middle of ten acres of woods. We used to open his gate all the time, then go on our way down the road. He'd spend an anxious hour or so hunting for us on his land, never finding us, of course. His own paranoid imagination was our best ally. This concept will work well with doors, too. Think about your mark finding open doors or windows in his house.

Genitals

I bet that few other books have a chapter with this title. A reader named Eric P. had an errant young woman do him a nasty once, and he hit back where her ego (alone?) showed.

"I got her worried about vaginal odor. She was vain as hell, insecure about her body, and very sensitive about 'personal things,' including body odors. I started by having a delivery service bring her a present of a gift-wrapped package of liquid douche, scented, of course. A few days later I put together an 'Emergency—Protect the Environment' package containing more products of a personal nature. I had that delivered. I sent a few cards from boys she knew and other friends hinting at this personal problem in broad terms, but never really mentioning vaginal odor, *per se.*

"I then had some memo pads and letterhead printed, using the name The Funky Vaginal Odor Control Board with a fake return address. I started sending these to her and getting friends from other cities to remail them for me. I posted her apartment door with an official-looking statement from the Board, using my letterhead.

"Next, I sent a couple of her boyfriends clothespins with instructions to clip on their noses when dating this girl because of her runaway case of vaginal odor.

"I did a few more things, but I guess you get the idea. In case any reader feels sympathy for the girl, don't. She deserved every single bit of trouble, believe me. I'll never collect what she owes me. But I'm trying to get back a little."

Another splendid addition to the genitals of a mark is spearmint oil. According to several Haydukers, most notably Dr. Schwatzen an Luft, if this elixir is placed on such sensitive areas as the genitals, the mark will really have the hots. The doctor suggests lubricating condoms with this oil or adding it to douching solutions, vibrators, or tampons. It will dry on the surface, then, when activated . . . call the fire department.

Graffiti

Bob from Everett, Washington, has a twist to the trick of writing your mark's (or his spouse's or sweetie's) name on restroom walls. Bob says to put just the phone number and no name, or use the real number and a made-up name. That last touch will make the spouse suspicious about extracurricular activities.

One of the goals the true graffiti artist strives for is permanency. You inscribe a message, and some diddlesquat civil servant or his lackey comes along and somehow covers or removes it. The Marquis de Amway has discovered a very good way to make graffiti last a lot longer on the job. Here's his idea.

"Let's say that someone has burned you, messed up your car, or otherwise marred your person or property, and you want to graffiti them back, but in such a way that the message will stick. If so, you're tuned to the right guy. Pay attention now.

"Get a piece of paper and spell out 'UP YOURS!' or 'YOUR WIFE SUCKS,' or some other very rude, personal grossity, using Comet or Ajax cleanser to spell the message. Then, spray over the whole thing with Right Guard, English Leather, or any of those sprays that will burn. Test them first. You can also use charcoal lighter or lighter fluid if you want to.

"Go to the home of the person you want to get back at, and tape the message paper to the floor, wall, even onto his car, or wherever you want the message to appear. Next, spray a stream of lighter fluid leading away from the paper, sort of like a fuse. Light that fuse and run like hell.

"WHOOSH, the paper blows up instantly, but there's no fire danger because everything just sort of disintegrates. But the cleanser chemically etches your rotten message onto whatever you stuck it to so well that it will never come off.

"There it is, your message, etched on permanently."

"We've tried it, and this stuff will work on concrete, metal, brick, tile, wood, anywhere. You can 'say' anything to anyone this way, and it will be damn near permanent," the Marquis de Amway tells me.

If it is inconvenient for you to write your graffiti on the spot, you can always use Avery labels, those adhesive-backed units that people use to address envelopes and so on. You can be as gross as you wish, and it takes only a few seconds to stick them into place. They are hard to remove, too.

Gun Control

Once, in another life, I was co-hosting a cutesy-tootsie cocktail party when an archetypical Loonie Liberal couple started passing around a "Ban the Guns" petition. Being a sensitive, polite sort even then, I quietly informed them that such political activity in my home offended me and would they please desist. Instead, I got more anti-gun pitch tinged with a hysteria about "our" being an elite group of opinion formers, whatever that is, and how vital it is that guns be banned. I was told this issue was more important than my own feelings.

My hand shot out, grabbed the petition, tore it in half then pitched both halves into the fireplace. I smiled and said, "Let the party continue, friends." From that point on, I have refused to party with activist Liberals or Conservatives. Neither are worth a bag of manure. I now party only with fellow drunks and heads.

But, my act of momentary violence was not really getting even. The petition destroying response was not the end of that party incident. After a cooling period, because like many activists, my anti-gun mark and his lady had limited attention spans, I started a little revenge campaign.

I bought some plastic handguns at a large discount store and began to place one in their mailbox or tape it to their apartment door at night every ten days or so. Once, I put one in on their car seat, then reported to police about "a car with a handgun on the seat in plain view." That created some real fun.

Using a postal money order I got my mark a year's membership in the National Rifle Association—faking the membership application a bit, of course. I pledged a huge amount in his name to all the "Right to Bear Arms" groups. He thus became the recipient of a large volume of mail particularly noxious to him.

He didn't change his mind, of course, but I heard through a third party that my mark was "furious" about someone harrassing him. But, he guessed "it was the price to pay for being controversial." To help his anxiety, I started doing the things on a more random basis—one month on, two off, one on, three off, two on, things like that.

The pro-gun baboons are just as bad, usually being illiterate as well. If you don't believe me, just read some of the letters in their various publications. I worry about some of them being allowed to drive cars, hold job, have children, and vote, much less owning firearms. But, I digress. . . .

A reader who farms wrote to tell me about having to chase slob hunters away from his house each and every deer season. A few give him a really bad time, which is why he reluctantly posted his 100 acres of prime woodland and lush cornfields. After one "sportsman" made a strong verbal threat backed with his rifle, my correspondent started his campaign. He got the hunter's vehicle license number and had a friend with the local police run down a name and address to go with it. It checked out.

"In addition to the usual goodies I picked up from your first book and used, I added a few of my own," this man wrote me. "I legally bought some submachine gun parts I saw advertised in a gun publication. At night I entered the man's backyard and buried the parts, wrapped in heavy plastic, in his garden.

'I knew this guy bragged how he could get guns for people without paperwork and at wholesale. So, I had a friend of mine who knows the gun business meet with the mark at a gun show and buy some handguns from him. There was no entrapment or strawman stuff—the mark sold illegally and outright for cash.

"I then called the regional BATF office and complained about what I had seen at the gunshow. You know the BATF! They gestapoized the mark. After the mark had gone through this and nearly had his entire collection confiscated by those federal nasties, I had another person tip our local police about the mark trafficking in machine guns. The tip included some information about the garden. You can imagine how that day dawned when the feds and the locals closed in on the mark.

What this man did was extreme and perhaps he overdid it. I have no love for the fascist swine at BATF. But, I also have no love for a slob who points a gun at someone else and/or threatens to use it. You takes your chances, as someone once pointed out.

Gun Nuts

The worst enemies that gun owners have are their own
rednecked mental peewees who write letters to *American
Rifleman* and *Gun Week* tying all the gun woes to liberals,
communists, and everything else in the world. They are the
single-minded adults whose entire lives revolve (no pun intended)
around the issue of gun control. Generally, they are from small
towns and have IQs to match. If only there were a way to keep
these bad examples out of the public media. Oh, well.

Bud Hammell is a gun collector who was harassed by the state
police because a fellow collector informed one of their agents that
Bud was selling guns to kids, didn't keep sales records, and so
on—all untrue. What had Bud really done? He had fairly outbid
Mr. Informant on a gun collection for sale. To get back at the jerk,
Bud waited a year, then placed some classified ads.

"I put the ads in controversial underground and radical
publications—both left and right wing. I advertised "Machine
Guns and Silencers for Sale . . . Cheap!"

In his ad, Bud made such clever claims as "I handle all red
tape—no forms for you to fill out, no expensive tax stamps . . . no
worry with the police or BATF."

Naturally, the name, address, telephone number, and dealer
number of Mr. Informant went on the bottom of the ad as its logo.

Mr. Informant was a licensed gun dealer, but he didn't have the proper license to sell machine guns or silencers. The ads had been out only a week when the first federal agent came to talk with Mr. Informant.

Ask anyone who is a licensed gun dealer or knows the business; it's really bad news to have these gun law feds on your case, especially if you *are* innocent. America's federal gun law cops are the nearest thing to the Gestapo we have.

Hawkers

Don't read this section unless you are (1) gross, (2) have a strong stomach, (3) have a terminally bizarre sense of humor, or (4) all of the above. Thanks to Chris Scott, we now have a creative use for hawkers. See, I warned you! Its not too late to turn back a few sentences. Very well.

Hawkers are especially yukky specimens of phlegm which one hawks up from the nether regions of the throat and the waste canals of the nasal passages. According to Scott, a hawker is an especially gooey mass of phlegm containing enough multicolored solids to make it an effective missile.

A dirty trickster can use hawkers in a plebian sense, or he may operate with some creative class. For example, it is possible, Scott tells me, to quietly deposit a few hawkers in glassware at cafeterias and restaurants. When an innocent customer selects the annointed vessel he will be horrified, sickened and will probably make this fact loudly known to your mark—the management of the restaurant.

In direct attack, which is not especially subtle and could invite physical retribution, the hawker is propelled directly upon the mark. Scott says that only choice hawkers should be used for this purpose and that a careful intelligence analysis should be made of the mark, the target area and setting. According to a former Major League baseball pitcher, one of his teammates was exceptionally adept at this trick, and once made another teammate physically sick by sloppily depositing and especially horrible mixture of hawker and chewing tobacco on the man's arm. The horrified teammate who received this offering ran for the bathroom and spent the next few minutes embracing the commode while spilling his lunch into the bowl.

Highways

An activist can have fun on the roadway, too. Can you imagine the damage possible if one were to substitute a road sign that read, GROSS WEIGHT 15 TONS, for the original sign on a bridge approach that read, GROSS LOAD 5 TONS? One protesting employee did this at his employer's Ohio plant and had materials shipments shut down for eight days.

In World War II, it was common for enemy agents on all sides to turn road signs so as to misdirect military convoys, screwing up operations. The same tactic could be used today, even if your only enemy is some governmental branch or agency.

In the annals of highway history no one has seen the equal of the many low points of the Pennsylvania Department of Transportation, traditionally a repository for political hacks, Mafia underlings, patronage hogtroughers, and the terminally incompetent. M. Harvey Shopp, a veteran political trickster, has all sorts of suggestions for highway fun such as painting sawhorses to look like official blockades and using them to close highways, bridges, etc.

Another of Shopp's ideas is to produce bogus DETOUR signs and place them at strategic locations where they will be sure to screw up highway traffic.

The road woes of Allen McDonald illustrate the rationale

behind these moves. Whenever the county in which he lived did road repair to a bridge near his home, they always parked their equipment in his yard. When county road scrapers went by, they piled a line of debris high enough to close his driveway. In winter, they also closed his own freshly shoveled driveway, this time with ice-hard snow and frozen slush. All calls to county officials were answered only with uncaring and operationally impotent cluckings of the tongue.

"I decided to return some of the favors," McDonald said. "I began to turn road and other directional signs around. I stole a couple of BRIDGE OUT signs in another county and placed them in front of perfectly good bridges in our county. I once called the local radio station and announced several road repairs that would mandate detours—telling them I was a county road super, of course—which really screwed up local traffic for a couple of days.

"The upshot is that the county got a lot of nasty calls and even more bad media publicity, and the county commissioners agreed to investigate these problems 'caused' by the road people. Naturally, in the midst of all this I also brought up my beefs about their conduct, offering to testify at the hearings. All abuses against my property quickly stopped. So I stopped my counter-abuse program.

Check the "Joggers" section of this book to learn about the use of the OSS tire spikes of World War II infamy.

Holidays

Our kindly charities would have you invite every deprived/depraved minority from boat people to orphans to democrats into your home for Christmas, birthdays, and other holidays. Down at the Louisiana School of Living Divinity, the Rev. Tobin Williams has an interesting alternative. He thinks it would be nice to invite some roadkill.

"Imagine the look on the mark's and his family's faces when they're gathered around the holiday tree or festive table as the posthumous guest of honor is unveiled—inside a gaily wrapped package.

"You need an opaque plastic bag, of course, so the mark or his designee will reach in and grab hold of the roadkill. It would also help if this bag is hermetically sealed to hold in the festive aroma until the very last minute.

"It goes without adding that this present must be appropriately gift-wrapped and carded," says Rev. Williams.

Homes

All sorts of things have homes—snails, snakes, groundhogs, weasels, Japanese beetles, even marks. One vengeful way of getting even with a mark is to destroy the moat to the castle of his/her home. The idea is to hit close to home, for both the physical and the psychological destruction involved.

One example started at the apartment of Pat Konely. Because the landlord refused to make needed roof repairs, several rainstorms flooded Konely's apartment, damaging personal property. The landlord also refused to pay damages, and Konely didn't have the money to fight the landlord's attorney.

Pat Konely admits the response wasn't very funny, but it did put a damper on the mark's day and his own home. It worked because the mark's front door had one of those mail slots cut in it. Konely says that this stunt works wonders when the mark is not aware of what's going on until the poor drip really gets the message. Here's what Konely suggests. Hook a hose, ideally the mark's, to the outdoor faucet. Unscrew the power nozzle so you have bare hose. Carry it to the mail slot and quietly fit the bare hose end through the slot and into the house. Got the picture? Good. Konely says you just turn on the faucet and hope the mark has slow reactions. Most tricksters would agree that it's hardly sporting to do this when the mark is away from home.

"That would be like shooting puppies in a barrel," Konely

snorts. "At least tip the barrel over and give them a running start, so to speak."

If your mark hates cats, be sure to place dead fish in obscure and unpleasant places around his/her abode. Do this at night. If you want feline audio accompaniment, tie a large dead fish from a tree limb or pole just out of the reach of the neighborhood cats. The nearer to the mark's bedroom window, the better.

The modern epoxy glues are a miracle to many and a menace to others. The latter is exemplified by the exasperation of a person who's just discovered that someone has squirted a load of strong glue into her/his door lock. (Liquid solder works too.)

You know all those vents in the back and top of a television set? If you ever pour a bunch of iron filings down in there, some interesting things will happen to the mark's set the next time it is turned on.

How about some party humor? If your mark doesn't know you're getting back at him yet, you might even find yourself a guest in the target home. You could start off your festivities by quieting yourself away from the crowd, locating the family freezer, and either turning the unit down greatly, pulling the plug (unless it's equipped with a safety signal), or switching it to defrost.

A trickster by the name of Micki related how she once came bearing gifts for the mark's family freezer. She had matched the hostess's freezer wrapping paper and style perfectly. Then, nestled among the nice beef roasts, steaks, hamburgers, and chickens belonging to the mark, Micki added her own packages of frozen roadkill—dead cats, small dogs, groundhogs, and crows.

Happy eating, all you mystery-meat fans.

While doing your tour of the targeted facilities don't forget to dump some fiberglass or insulation dust into the mark's washing machine. It will be picked up by the clothes, ideally undergarments. Within half an hour of getting dressed, a person wearing clothing impregnated by the fiberglass or insulation dust will wish he/she weren't. It creates terrible itching that takes two or three days to disappear. The best part is that no one ever thinks to blame the rash on sabotaged clothing. Repeated doses of this stunt are enough to make a strong mark crumble. A continual supply of "product" is assured if you mix the nasty dust in with the laundry detergent.

Every real kid knows what sulfur smells like when burned—horribly rotten eggs. Once, some of my peer-group delinquents put three pounds of it in a nasty neighbor's furnace, after somehow gaining entry to the basement. The house had to be aired for nearly forty-eight hours. It was awesome. If you want some fireworks with your sulfur-in-the furnace gimmick, throw in a mixture of potassium permanganate and sugar. It will flare, smoke grandly, and, with the sulfur present, stink all the more.

Here is one of Leon Spectre's recipes for ill humor. He hopes you dig it.

Your mark (and family if there is one) is away for at least the weekend, and you know about it enough ahead that you can hire a backhoe operator. Also, rent a pickup truck and tape a cardboard sign to its door with some vague identification on it about a landscaping business. Smear the license plate with mud or borrow another plate for a short while.

You should arrive at the mark's house about half an hour before the backhoe. Naturally, you used the mark's name when you engaged the backhoe and you told the operator you'd have a landscape contractor (you) there to meet him. The neighbors should think everything is in order if you act as if you know what you're doing.

Don't give the backhoe operator a good look at you, and use some disguise kit if possible. The premise is that the mark wants to add a basement room somewhere on the house. You must tell the backhoe operator exactly where to excavate. In most suburban areas, underground utility lines are indicated with aboveground markers. You can pick up gas lines and water lines from the meters. Pick an area clear of utility lines and pipes and lay out some string and stakes. Do all this before your operator arrives. Tell him your client, the mark, wants that area excavated and to bill the mark directly. Further, tell him that you have to leave to pick up your foreman and crew and that you'll be back in about twenty minutes. Ideally, you'll never see the backhoe operator again.

As Frank Foge points out, "My chemistry teacher always said there'd be a practical use for these high school science courses someday." She was right. Do you remember what termites look like? Good. If not, any insect book will tell you. Or visit your local Orkin man and tell him you need to obtain some termite eggs for an experiment. Or get them from a science-supply house.

I bet you already know the experiment. It's called how fast can the little eggs hatch into hungry termites and devour the mark's house? There's no trick here; you just infest your mark's home with the little buggers. They'll do the rest. This last one was prompted by a frustrated renter whose landlady refused to have the cockroaches and other pests exterminated from an apartment. A serious illness to an infant child, traced directly to the landlady's refusal to follow sanitary laws, triggered the nasty "bugging" by the renter.

Hot Tubs

Carolyn, another L.A. punk rocker, says she once dumped five pounds of fertilizer in a self-styled Lothario's jacuzzi. The resulting odor was quite vulgar throughout the entire apartment complex. Another friend, Mel Cajones, says that someone entering a hot tub or jacuzzi containing this fertilizer broth is quite likely to get nasty skin burns.

I'm not so sure about this one, but as it came in from our very wonderful Heidi Marie, why not try it? After a particularly unhappy party experience involving a hot tub and some very obnoxious people, a friend of Heidi's decided to stiffen up the host's hot tub—symbolically, no doubt. She added several boxes of cream of rice cereal to the tub. It sounds great, something to interest a lot of kids . . . a huge bowl of hot cream of rice cereal.

Hotels, Motels, and High Rises

This one came in from Gabe Torquato because he was angry at a hotel that quartered him in a room directly above the grand ballroom where a convention of vets was trying to sound like the Battle of the Bulgies. His revenge was so simplistic and slapstick that I was not going to use it. But, the sillier it got, the more impressive the idea became. Read on.

His original idea was to go to random room areas of the hotel and drop large plastic bags of water out of windows on convention delegates. Simple stuff—most high school kids are veterans of that one. But, I began to think about deeper implications. Suppose you add rubber toy rats or snakes to the bag of liquid? Suppose you use urine? Suppose you mixed feces in with the water? Suppose you mixed in canned vegetable soup, so it would look like vomit? Or, you could jettison bags of paint. Or bags of exceptionally overripe roadkill.

While your primary mark is the hotel management, you are, of course, inflicting severe emotional distress upon those poor random targets down below. As the pain and shock of getting hit with a God-knows-what builds, so will the paranoia of "Why Me? Why Was I Chosen for This Attack.?"

One of Aunt Bertie's nephews told me about this one. He was staying at a motel in Memphis (sounds like a rock song title) on the same floor as a convention of very uptight Bible Bangers who spent half his sleepless night trying to save him, and praying for his lost soul. Actually, all he had lost by then was a night's sleep and his patience. The management merely "tut-tutted" a feeble apology, but refused to enforce quiet on the Lord's people.

The next morning, before checking out, Aunt Bertie's nephew used a razorblade to cut a small hiding hole into the pages of the Gideon Bible in his room. Closed, it looked like any other Bible. Open it up and you'll find two packets of condoms that dear nephew stashed there, along with a note "from" the Motel Management, written on a memo pad he'd filched at the desk during his nighttime complaint session. The note told the religious folks to use the rubbers to "get it up so they could get it on with a really religious experience." He signed it, "St. Peter, lay minister, order of St. Mattress."

A traveling man, the dear nephew has done the same basic trick to other motels which displease him, sometimes substituting dope, booze, porno, a guide to local hookers or gay bars for the condoms.

"Once I went to a blue-nosed, fundamentalist 'temple' and taped porno pictures in the church itself. I loved it and I bet some of the good parishioners did too on the next Sunday," he recalled.

Ahh yes, do unto others after they have done unto you. But, doeth yours twice as hard and nasty!

House Plants

I have this friend named Pangle, whose bossy roommate used to bitch all the time because Pangle would forget to water roomie's plants while roomie was out playing Jacques Cousteau on some friend's sailboat. Pangle figured the old salt needed some rubbing in, so she began to carry out the orders of her admirable roommate. She used salt water, a look of total innocence, then feigned sorrow when the plants failed to survive the saline watering voyage.

Along the same line, getting to the root of a personality conflict, one obviously henpecked reader noted that his domineering mother used to force him to keep her house plants cleaned, watered and cared for. He hated the plants, which is probably unfair, because I suspect it was his mother he really didn't like. Anyway, he started to mix food coloring in with the water he used on the plants.

"Within a week my mother had plants with colored 'veins' running through the stems and leaves. I convinced her they were very sick plants. She dismissed my care as incompetent and took over herself. That's all I needed."

He added a postscript that the plants died. His mother bought all new specimens and would not allow junior near them. I wondered as I read his letter again if he ever thought of putting food coloring in his mother's drinks.

Households

Kenny Braun had a nice little puppy that he kept in a roomy, chicken wire enclosure of some 200 square feet with a solid, comfortable doghouse in the center. He fed and watered his pup daily, and his kids played with it a lot. It had a great life in its little environment.

Then, there was the next door neighbor, Lorrie Miller, who had a big, bully, nasty Doberman that had to live up to its reputation. It used to trespass into Braun's place and terrorize both the kids and the puppy. After many wasted attempts to dissuade Miller from this folly, Braun took other action.

"I filled a balloon with urine, then went next door and hurled it though the screen door so it would splatter all over the new carpet inside on the living room. The Doberman came loping into the room, sniffed my splashy results, and started 'marking' all over the carpet area, trying to reestablish his territory."

If you need a lesson on dog territoriality, they mark the boarders of their property by spraying copious amounts of urine. Ever see a dog hit a tree or a bush? They are usually marking territory. Needless to say, the Miller dog spent days trying to overcome Braun's repeated urine-filled balloon attacks. Soon, the expensive new carpet fell victim to this odorous and acidic assault. The Doberman got full credit, and was soon penned up. Such is a dog's life.

Hunters

Amazing as it may seem, a lot of people don't like hunters who act like mindless killers or slobs. Let's go for the jerk who happens to be a hunter or whose hunting has caused you enough grief to want to get even. Jimi the Z sneaks his marvelous madness into the field here.

"Once it was imperative that I return some disfavor to a person who hunted. I caused him to receive some custom-loaded shotgun shells. Instead of the usual shot, we loaded the shells with a combination of corrosive salts, coarse sand, tiny lead balls covered with grinding compound, plus steel burrs. We also used flammable padding instead of the normal plastic wadding. You wouldn't believe what a day of shooting those special loads did to the man's shotgun and what *that* did to the man's psyche and budget."

IRS

A veteran dirty trickster named Michael Mertz has something good to say about the Internal Revenue Service—it can be used to furnish a hard time for your mark. Mertz knows his way around government agencies, and here's one of his IRS offerings.

"You'll need your mark's Social Security number and some other obvious personal data. Once you get those data you're on your way.

"Call a regional IRS office and 'confess' that you have cheated on your income tax, your conscience has bothered you, and you want to make things right by this great nation. Make an appointment with an auditor, using your mark's name, Social Security number, address, etc."

The kicker comes when the mark doesn't show up to keep the appointment, for obvious reasons. The IRS will send a visitor around to talk with the mark, and chances are he will be audited, regardless of his explanations.

So much for using IRS to hassle your mark. Many more folks would prefer the IRS were the mark. As in dealing with any large bureaucracy and its people, many of the stunts mentioned in other chapters may be brought to play against the IRS. However, there are a few specific tricks that might be used to bring rain on the IRS picnic.

You could start by picking up a bunch of blank returns and filing them in the names of your least favorite people. I have been assured by a former IRS field auditor that someone will have to make an effort to verify each return.

With the help of your printer and your newly found forgery skills, prepare some financial documents indicating that some person or corporation has received some substantial income. Make copies of copies several times until you have a fifth- or sixth-generation copy that is not too clean but is still easily sharp enough to read. The idea is to make it look like copies of a purloined original. Call an IRS office from a phone booth and tell them you are an honest employee of the mark and you think he is evading taxes. Offer to send the IRS person the papers. Get off the phone very quickly, then send the papers. If the IRS gets nasty they may find themselves in court. I got this idea from a man who worked for a company that did fight IRS in court and won big—through an honest IRS error. Think what could happen to IRS if you fed them a dishonest error!

Joggers

Overweight and overwrought motorists drive by in their Detroit Dinosaurs, pass a jogger, and mutter, "Damn stupid schmuck." It's the human way to hate what and whom you don't understand. Joggers are often thought of as nuts, oddballs, and kooks to be dealt with.

Marty Jones, a landowner, is more specific, saying, "They run across a corner of my property, using a path I put in for my own use. I posted the land, but they ignored the postings. I have tried to talk to them, but they may or may not even stop to listen. If they stop they keep running in place while I'm raising hell about trespass. I think most joggers are rude, self-centered, and selfish. I was thinking about hiding in the bushes and ambushing them with my kid's BB gun."

For a variety of reasons, many people don't like joggers. Some folks even actively plot against joggers, using cars and motorcycles, then arming themselves with boards, pies, and other objects with which to strike the runners. There are less barbaric ways, however.

Tire spikes are a World War II relic. During the hostilities, they were dumped from low-flying aircraft onto enemy airfields and main transportation roadways, where they caused havoc. Your use might not be so widespread, but with equally exasperating results. The tire spike is a simply made piece of one-eighth-inch-thick steel cut in the form of a four-pointed star. Its purpose is to puncture rubber tires. The original wartime models were three inches in diameter and had four points at forty-five-degree angles. One of the points always stuck upward, ready to impale a vehicle tire. Even today, there are many uses for tire spikes.

One anti-jogger has already suggested that these spikes be reduced in size and dropped strategically near the running habitat of these long-range exercise buffs. The purpose, I presume, is to penetrate the expensive bottom of expensive jogging footwear and, perhaps, the expensive foot of the jogger. One critic called this tactic "a really sick pain in the metatarsus."

Ultrathin piano wire strung shin high on a pathway is excruciatingly nasty. That's another World War II stunt redrafted for this book by Colonel Jake Mothra. Many military manuals offer equipment and directions, he adds.

Another contribution to joggermania would be to sprinkle marbles on their special little pathways. Another nasty trickster, Hidell Crafard, told me about an acquaintance at the Hunt Sporting Club in Dallas who actually put ground glass into the running shoe of a bitter enemy. Perhaps that's where filet of sole originated.

There aren't many counteractivities a jogger can use in retaliation. One is to carry MACE for obvious use. Another tactic is to carry cans of garish-hued spray paint. These can be directed against attackers' automobiles.

Landlords

Their landlord kicked a couple of my readers out, claiming they had violated the lease by holding "loud parties." The landlord's complainant was an eighty-one-year-old neighbor lady who was partially deaf and totally bigoted. Her eyesight was good enough, though, to note that the couple renting was a salt 'n' pepper pair. There had been no loud parties. In fact, there were no parties at all. A quiet couple, their socializing was limited to two or three other couples coming in for bridge once or twice a month. Ho hum.

Not wanting to fight in court, they found another apartment, then decided to fight back their own way. They waited a few months and learned through good intelligence sources that the landlord would be away for a weekend.

They called a caterer and arranged a very posh affair, ordering full service, the best in food, expensive lawn furniture, a strolling band, champagne fountain, silver and crystal . . . the whole bit. All arrangements were handled by telephone. Invitations went out to all sorts of people, including bar derelicts, plenty of minorities, neighbors of the landlord, and, of course, to add to the cover, every present and former tenant they could locate. It was timed for noon Sunday. The landlord was due home by four that afternoon.

Times were tough, and the caterer was only too glad to get the business. Yet can you imagine the business the mark found when he returned home that Sunday afternoon with "his" party in full and very expensive swing? Naturally, all the guests greeted him with thrilled smiles, also asking when he'd open up the house so they could use the bathrooms.

Sputter, sputter, sputter went the landlord. His wife went wonder, wonder, wonder. The caterer went pay, pay, pay. The salt 'n' peppers went ho, ho, ho.

A variation of this same idea was suggested to me by Lynn in Denver. In both her case and the one just mentioned, the vengeance was most fitting, plus being most expensively and emotionally successful.

Not all landlords are as wonderful as you've been reading about. Bob Pursell, who used to live in Boston, told me about an apartment owner who had a "no paint" complex until the kids who were his tenants agreed to paint the place if the landlord bought the paint. The agreement was made.

"The kids painted everything black. I mean everything," Bob related. "They painted the toilets black. They even shut off the water in them, dried out the bowls, and painted the insides of the commodes black. Even the light bulbs were black. The windows were black. If you can think of anything else, they did too, and painted it black. The ceiling was black, the beds were black . . . everything was black . . . except the landlord's face. It was red."

A Chicago journalist told me about his undergraduate days when his landlord refused to fix a septic tank overflow. The smell and the hygiene got worse, and as summer approached, when school ended, the students living in that rental sewer were only too happy to get out.

"We left him a little overflow message of our own about the need to clean up his sewerage. We got back our security deposit and just before leaving, one of the guys, who'd hidden, flushed twenty pounds of powdered detergent down the toilet. We then left, immediately."

Land Rapists

Rooters of the lost ark will appreciate this version of the
Piltdown Man. It's a creative way to harass those land rapists
who anti-semantically call themselves "developers." You go to
the work site when it is dark or otherwise unobserved. You bury
some objects like arrow heads, odd pottery shards, human skulls
snitched from a bio classroom, and other artifacts. The best way to
proceed is to tip off some serious college kids who like to work
on digs. Females are usually best for this role as they are more
often true believers about this sort of "discovery." Let these kids
discover your "artifacts." Hype the find through the local
newspaper—especially smaller weeklies. Insist through the local
historical society that moral and legal pressure be brought down
on the developer to halt his operations until a scientific dig can
verify the findings.

Laundromats

Recently, I listened as a young woman related how her roommate would continually come in from drunken orgies, sick to her stomach because of what she had done. On one occasion, she managed to void the contents of her stomach all over the work wardrobe of the young lady telling the story. Apparently, it was not the first time it had happened.

"I pleaded with her to stop getting loaded like that and making it with any guy who asked, usually right in our room while I was there in my bed. I threatened to move out. She was a nice kid, sometimes, but this was the last humiliation and ruination for me and for my clothes. I moved out . . . but that wasn't all. I had to get even.

"A week or so later, when I knew she'd do her laundry, I put my plan into action. After she put her clothes into the dryer and went next door for coffee, I slipped into the laundry room unnoticed and tossed a handful of colorful wax crayons into the dryer with her clothes."

Joseph and his Biblically mentioned coat had nothing on this boozy sex-date.

From our quickie, but itchy, division, if you want to give a person a really uncomfortable day, toss a piece of fiberglass in with wash containing your mark's undergarments. It's guaranteed to ruin his day and, with luck, could also provide a mild rash.

Lawns and Gardens

This is a simple and effective hit'n run tactic to have fun with your mark's lawn. Everytime you walk or drive by the mark's yard, throw a few large stones on the lawn. It all builds up. Vary the size, and you'll not only ruin his mower blade, but you might even get him to sail one or more of these stone missiles through a window or into his car.

I know one friend of the environment who live-traps his Japanese beetles, then at night takes his catch over to his mark's yard and garden and sets the little buggers loose to do their misdeeds there. A refinement of this was suggested by Bob Thornbroug who says to plant Japanese beetle traps in your mark's garden but take the catch bags off the traps.

Scattering weed seeds and other vegetative miscreants into his mark's finely tuned yard is Sid Nerko's way of getting back at manicured lawn freaks.

Lawsuits

According to one lawyer who really does have the Establishment Bar Association stamp of approval, it's fairly easy for you to sue someone. Most states have something called a small claims or citizen's court for just such actions. But you also have individual access to regular state and federal courts, just like those lawyers in the cash-green, six-piece suits. The Hayduke legal adviser says you should go to your local law library and/or courthouse to read some of the books on the topic which legally interests you or in which you wish to sue.

The law library has a set of books containing the exact legal forms necessary to sue someone. Find what you need and have a copy made or purchase a form. Don't be shy about asking lawyers—especially young ones who pop into the room—for advice and help. Don't be afraid to ask a clerk for help, either. Fill in the blanks on the form, asking for help if you need it, and file your suit with the clerk. It will cost you from nothing to about fifty dollars to file a suit.

With that modest investment of your time and money, you can file damages asking for hundreds of thousands of dollars. Think of the stress value and the bad publicity your suit will cause the mark, as you see how surprisingly easy it is to institute a lawsuit.

What if *you* should get sued? Easy. Go to the courthouse and countersue. Most people don't think of that. That's why there are so many losers and so many lawyers out there. Do it yourself.

Libraries

Juan McMann didn't even own a library card. He'd never ever been in the library. Yet, he received an overdue book/fine letter from the very same library he'd never been in. His telephoned explanations were abused and he was insulted. He was threatened again. He finally had to spend $50 to hire an attorney to set the record straight. He cursed the damn library.

Juan spent another $50 having some bookplates printed. Bookplates are snobbish gum-backed labels that announce a book's title, author and donor. Juan had some very pornographic, bogus bookplates printed, and pasted them in old classics at his favorite library. I will leave to your imagination just how clinically disgusting his choices were. He's a very grossly creative man, and his specific ideas don't belong in a book of this nature.

Do yours?

License Plates

There are many sophisticated and clever ways to obtain additional vehicular license plates that aren't registered in your real name. However, it's not necessary to fool around with all that esoterica. Be like a street punk and simply steal what you need. A bad guy who needs a plate simply removes one from someone's car or truck. That simple. This is also highly illegal. But if you're careful and use a bit of common sense, can you think of a simpler and safer way of getting the extra plates you need for dirty tricks?

Locks

Several readers complained that when they tried to pump Epoxy into locks using a pressure gun or a syringe, the stuff hardened unless they used it quickly. One of my favorite friends and chemist came up with the no-pun solution. Gino Sanford suggests mixing the Epoxy with some form of alcohol before putting the stuff into the syringe, He says many alcohols will work to retard the curing process until you're ready to use it. The exposure to air will start the evaporation of the alcohol and the curing of the Epoxy.

Mafia

The Mob is like the weather in that everyone talks about it, but. .
. . Everyone knows someone in La Cosa Nostra, right? Every Italian
family semibrags of an uncle, cousin, or someone not too close,
who's connected, right? At best, the contact is a numbers runner.
Usually, it's some holster-sniffing braggart who drinks coffee in the
same shop the local organization's soldiers do. But, as Marshall
McLuhan taught, reality doesn't matter, it's what people think.

Marcia Springchurch is a good friend of mine who once had a
problem with a male subordinate. He refused to take orders from a
woman. He got nasty and started the usual dirty lies about how a
gorgeous young woman gets into an executive position so quickly.
Marcia is a very clever lady in the vengeance area.

She made a pre-arranged telephone call to another friend, making
her end of the conversation seem as if she were talking to some
Mob enforcer. She knew her problem-boy was listening to her as his
desk was less than a dozen feet away. She did a poor *sotto voce* bit
of trying to hide what she wanted, but made it clear she wanted
some "contract work done." She glanced at her mark, acted shocked
that he was listening, mumbled something about "can't talk now,"
and hung up. She looked flushed and left the room. A seed of
paranoia was planted in his pea-sized brain.

Starting that weekend, two door-filling hulks called on the
troublemaker in his apartment, at his favorite disco bar and once,
after work in the company parking lot. They made it very clear that

his lies about his female boss had displeased someone very powerful and important. They told him he was an unimportant worm that nobody would miss. They gave him two weeks to get a new job and get out of town, while he could still do so without the aid of an ambulance.

"It's gonna be tough for you to do the kinda work you do, pal, if we hafta come back and rip your arms out at the shoulder. And we will, we will," they told the quaking mark.

He beat their deadline by a week.

You should know that Marcia's two heavies were not really Mob muscle. They were a couple of her out of town friends who gleefully agreed to play the role. They made no illegal threats in front of witnesses, nor did they carry weapons. They simply looked, dressed and played the role of what people think a Mob musclepower soldier is supposed to look and act like.

As a postscript, Marcia says that a real Mob type she really did know found out about her actors and thought it was a hilarious scheme. He also told her that he would have made a couple of his boys—the real thing—available if necessary.

Mannequins

Store mannequins can be recruited into your dirty tricks army to frighten deserving marks. Attend a going-out-of-business sale and buy the store mannequins. You can dress them in Salvation Army, Goodwill, or thrift shop clothing. Or, leave them naked if your mission would benefit from that style of exposure. You can use these silent sentinels for all sorts of vengeful mischief.

In one instance, a reader of the first volume reported to me that he terrorized a lawyer who had screwed him out of money in a will probate case. The reader placed naked mannequins on the mark's lawn, in his car and in the hallway outside his office. He mutilated the genital areas and wrote voodoo symbols and occult signs on the bodies of the store dummies using runny red paint for blood. He made-up the faces to look like that of the lawyer and his family. The harried lawyer finally went to the police, totally convinced a dangerous lunatic was after him.

Marriage

Carol Sludge and a friend decided they should stage manage an entire wedding for a mark. So they did. She handled the gown and the bridesmaids' goodies, and he did the sartorial bit for the men. They got invitations and arranged for a church, a reception hail, a caterer, and an orchestra. They did it all in the name of the mark and his fictitious spouse to be. They chose a time when the mark was on vacation to send out invitations for the Sunday the mark was due back in town. Everyone showed up for the ceremony—everyone but the "bride and groom." Guests were somewhat miffed, and merchants and others descended upon the mark at his place of business Monday morning, wanting to be paid for goods and services.

Beyond that, what do you turn to after the standard old buns of wrecking the marriage ceremony have been batted around the bachelor-party table? Here are some quickie suggestions, brought to you by the Reverend Robby Gayer:

1. Hire a woebegone lady with a young child to troop into the reception and confront the groom-mark with the question of his continued child-support payments.

2. Hire an outstandingly healthy young wench who is just brimming over with sensual physical charm. She should cause heads to turn if she's costumed correctly as she vamps up to the groom-mark and plants wet soul kisses on him, cooing,

"Don't forget our past, love. And when you're tired of that little girl next-door, you know where to find me." As she leaves, she stage whispers, "Last [night, week, whatever] was just super. Don't be a stranger—you're too much man for that."

3. Call the church office before the ceremony and say that a crazed ex-lover of the bride plans to destroy the reception. Just as the reception begins, arrange to have many M80s or grenade simulators exploded.

4. Consider bringing additives into play with the punch and the food.

5. Hire someone, grief stricken at the loss of the bride or groom, to messily and dramatically "attempt suicide" at either the ceremony or the reception. Be sure to have associates to carry the victim out quickly for "medical

6. Hire someone to become physically sick during the ceremony or the reception. With luck, you can get a member of the wedding party to do this.

7. Use many additives in the groom-mark's drinks during the prenuptial bachelor party.

8. Hire someone to slowly and dramatically flash the minister from the back of the church while everyone else is facing front. This also works well if there is a singer in the choir balcony. Try to upset him or her during a song.

9. Call the state police or the drug-enforcement people and give them a complete description of the car that will carry the bridal couple on the honeymoon. Report that the couple and the car are really dope mules, that is, couriers of the drug trade.

Mass Transit

I don't know how useful this is, but someone named Terry the Tramp, who says he used to ride with Hell's Angels, related that you can make a hellish sound, and shake up the citizens, not to mention the driver, by rolling a large, metal trash can under the wheels of a city bus.

"It makes a sound like a real bad accident, man," he said. "It sounds like one of the little compact cars got crunched by the bus, run over, then dragged along."

It works best at dusk or during the first half light of early morning rush hour. I bet if you added a few "bloody" mannequins to the mess you could increase the scene's tensions.

Media

The mass media—newspapers, radio, television, and magazines—can be helpful tools in getting even, or they can be your mark in a dirty trick. I suggest you keep your media-as-tool aspect relegated to local events and local media. In general, newspapers tend to be conservative and stodgy and not much interested in your rousing of the rabble. Most newspaper officials play golf with corporate officials, and their common bonds are advertising and profits.

Television likes good, visual consumer stories, and local TV stations will go for local controversy more often than will local newspapers. Here are some basic suggestions for using the media to help you in your getting-even campaigns.

If the editor says the event is news, then it goes out to the public as news. People don't make news; editors make news.

To impress editors you have to keep coming up with fresh action. You have to be visual, outrageous, funny, controversial, and brief. Your message has to be catchy, visual, and packaged to fit ninety seconds of time in the six- or eleven-o'clock news slot. It's no wonder longwinded academics end up with "Viewpoint," or "Talk Out" at 3:00 o'clock Monday morning. They don't know how to use TV.

Now, how do you get even with the media when they deserve it? There are several things you can do:

- Take or phone in a fake wedding story, being sure to give them a legitimate-looking bride-groom photo. It doesn't matter who the people in the picture really are. Most smaller and medium-sized papers will publish without checking, which could lead to all sorts of wonderful things if you've been inventive in your choice of marriage partners.
- Use a low-power mobile transmitter to add little bits of original programming to your community's commercial radio station. Some people did this in Syracuse, New York, and drove officials crazy with hilariously obscene fake commercials, news bulletins, etc.
- Newspapers often have huge rolls of newsprint in relatively unsecured storage areas. It is a low-risk mission to insert paper-destroying insects or chemicals into those rolls.
- Some small radio stations are often loosely attended at night. Often, only the on-duty DJ is around, and even he will have to go to the can sometime. You might be able to wait until then or to have an accomplice distract that DJ while you place a prerecorded cassette with a message of your own choosing on the air.
- With smaller newspapers, it is sometimes easy to get phony stories and/or pictures published. Using your imagination, you can certainly cause a variety of grief for a variety of reasons. Be sure to match your cure with their crime.

According to media consultant Jed Billet, if you have a financially weak radio station in your area, you can often place ads for your mark over the telephone. Agreeing, Eugene Barnes recalls, "A couple of years ago, I wanted to get back at a doctor who'd really screwed up my family with some terrible behavior in a business dealing. So I designated him as my mark and had him 'open a pizza business.' I called the radio station and had them run a saturation campaign of twenty-five spots per day listing his name and home address and telephone number, plus all sorts of promotional gimmicks, like free delivery, free Coke, stuff like that. He had to have his telephone disconnected for a week. The station ran the ads for a day and a half before the doctor got them pulled. He had 'customers' off and on, though, for the next ten days."

Newspapers, magazines, radio, and TV are businesses, very concerned about their profit-and-loss statements. Sales, both of advertising and of audience for that advertising, are vital to the media. Knowing this, old media hand Ben Bulova has a scheme that works well most of the time.

"Most newspapers will start a subscription with a telephone call," Bulova says. You call in and order a subscription in your mark's name and address."

The next step, Bulova explains, is to call the mark and, using the real circulation manager's name, tell him that you are with the circulation department of the newspaper and that they're going to give the mark a free trial subscription. That way, when the papers start to arrive, the mark thinks they're free. When the bill arrives, the mark will call the real circulation person. That conversation would be interesting to overhear.

Bulova says that this will work with magazines and trade publications, as well. He advocates an entire string of such gifts.

Medical

Neil Nixon had this nasty neighbor we'll call William F. Smith. Smith's dog was almost as ugly as its owner, especially in temperament. The major difference between the two was that the dog didn't have acne scars. One day the dog attacked and bit Neil Nixon, after crossing two yards to get at our correspondent. The attack was totally unprovoked and obviously unwelcomed. Let's pick up Neil's account (and accounting) of the matter.

"I got some nasty wounds and a fair-sized scar on my leg. I decided to bite back at Smith's ego. I got a medical association letterhead by taking a junk mail piece soliciting research fund support, then making a clean letterhead from it with a Xerox machine. The resultant copy looked just like clean, new letterhead.

"I then used a public typewriter to send him the following letter, slightly revised copies of which I also sent to his wife, employer, and closest business associates, asking for their help in persuading Smith to come out of his sacred closet."

Neil's letter read:

As the leading publisher of medical books dealing with unusual problems, we will offer you $50 if you will allow our photographer to picture your barnaclelike acne condition which is of considerable interest to our readers.

You and your condition were brought to our attention by (name mark's doctor) whose nurse told some of her friends about you. They have described the gross appearance of this advanced stage of acne and suggested we contact you. We are also contacting your close friends and business associates in hopes that they might help convince you to share your sorrow with others, all in the interest of medical science, of course.

Memoranda

Memoranda are part of the interoffice political warfare of everyone who happens to be branded with professional or clerical-level employment. Many memos are written in the tradition of Cover Your Ass (CYA), while a lot of other memos are written because of the insecurity of the writer. Or when some memos are written, they cause insecurity in those who must read them. All this pedagogical pap about memoranda will serve a purpose since memos may be used as weapons.

Let's say your mark has been shafting you during the interoffice status rivalry game. Or he or she has been taking credit for your good ideas and/or blaming you for his or her duds. Depending on the mark's personality, you might want to intercept one of his/her memos before it goes out, hold it a day, then send it back with some horrible message scrawled at the bottom or in the margin. Put some honcho's initials on it. Be careful, though, of handwriting here. Or you may simply want to destroy the outgoing memo, or destroy the response memo, or cause copies of sensitive memos to go to the wrong people. You can easily direct this person's fortune by manipulating his or her memo flow to the wrong people.

Mind and Ego Busters

Select a magazine with a large picture of a face on the cover. With a cigarette or match, burn out just the eyes and the mouth. Mail the magazine to your mark. Do this several times a month at random periods. It is a very eerie experience, according to Dirty Donna, who says she really knows the depths of this psycho-warfare. She didn't say she was a witch. But. . . .

Dirty Donna says that she also once sent a sympathy card to her mark's wife. Inside the card she wrote a personal message, "So terribly sorry to hear about your husband's untimely death." She dated the message two weeks in the future and mailed it that day. The date of the death was timed to coincide with the date of their wedding anniversary.

Money

Hedley Herndon from L.A. says that if you can get hold of some counterfeit money you should make sure that your mark gets some, too. This works well if the mark gets drunk and becomes loud, rowdy, and tosses his funny money around like there is no tomorrow. Guess again, folks, there is a tomorrow for your mark—in the federal pen.

Mooning

Shooting moons is a wonderful experience, as many readers have pointed out. Becky Beaver, a famous writer, has done it all over Ohio and Pennsylvania, as her ass is better looking than and as famous as her byline. But there have been a lot of other famous moonshots, according to the mail I get from readers.

Here are some extracts:

- When some prominent mark dies or some other deserving soul gets dead by circumstances which the TV cameras will cover, be sure and moon the funeral ceremony in the semidistant background just when and where the TV cameras are rolling. Maybe the TV editors will miss seeing you. Viewers won't miss it, though.
- Seek out some cult religious organization with a gathering or some uptight graduation ceremony. Moon it.
- Hover around family vacation sites of the type that attract typical American families. Moon them on the freeways, aiming for the backs of their cars, usually out your front window. These moon shots are great because the still fun 'n' innocent all-American kids in the car see your ass before their uptight, pucker-assed American parents do. The kids laugh. Kids are neat. Mooning is neat. Parents usually are not neat. It's hard to imagine that they were ever kids.

Movie Theaters

Saul Nerkmeister was annoyed as hell when he had to sit through a movie with a bunch of teenie punkers who talked, whispered, giggled, smoked, then noisily ate candy from crinkly paper bags. He complained to the ticket kid—a shaved-head clone of the punkers—who just smiled vacuously. Saul came back the following week to take his revenge.

The same gang was at this movie, too. Saul had borrowed a friend's bratty baby, who cried and cried loudly throughout the film. Saul, who had target shooter's ear plugs in his ears, had a jolly old time. He couldn't even hear the punkers cursing him and the baby.

Municipal Services

A former CIA operative who specialized in sabotage shared a couple of theoretical ideas about some cheap tricks. He suggests that if a municipality has corroded you with its parking corruption, then a return is only fair. He suggests a squirt or two of concentrated battery acid into a parking-meter slot. Repeat as necessary, he adds.

He has an excellent caveat to go with this, though: "If you do this sort of thing needlessly and unprovoked, it is nothing more than criminal vandalism, which is stupid, and you deserve what you get if you're caught.

"But, if you're doing it as a justified retaliation for something unjustified which was done to you and for which you have no other recourse, then give it your best shot."

You can also put epoxy or similar glue into that parking-meter slot, but that is readily visible. Another idea, according to Billy Bellan, is to screw up the meter so that it might still accept a few more coins but not operate any more. That way, more citizens get tickets because of an inoperable meter. There is more fuss and confusion for the authorities this way. He suggests that small washers coated with liquid solder or glue be placed in the meter slot.

A few sawhorses and some official-looking signs can close down a busy road. Set them up just before rush hour, and you will create chaos. If you do it well, it will be an hour before the mess is settled and things are back to semi-normal.

You know how public-employee unions are? Call the head of one union or some shop steward in your city or county. Say you are some big honcho—like a commissioner or a councilperson. Just raise royal hell. Get personal and abusive about some issue that's in the news. Try to provoke the person you are talking to. Faced with the call later, the official will honestly deny everything. Given the state of management-union relations at the moment, I doubt that many union folks will believe the management person you impersonated.

If the union is your mark, pick up some identification— credit cards, fake license, or something else that would document that you are the selected union official. Go to some municipal facility and pull off one of the dirty tricks mentioned in this book. On your way out, "accidentally" drop your mark's ID at the scene.

Never turn in false fire alarms. Fire is a serious business, and most firemen are volunteers who do a helluva job protecting you and the rest of your community. I have a lot of respect for firemen. Don't mess with them or their functions.

Usually, this is true of police, too, unless you happen to run into neo-Nazi stormtroopers on the force. For some reason police work can attract the town bully. Maybe it's the guns, uniforms, saps, and the power of the badge that draw them in. But as any good cop will tell you—they get more than their share of hoods.

It's cool to screw up the hoods in uniform. But stay off the cases of the good cops. They are decent people with tough enough jobs. The life of a cop is a hundred times tougher in many ways than your job. Stick to selective targeting here.

If you do have a badass cop or two it might be fun to chain

the afflicted black-and-white to the car parked behind it or to something that will cause damage, à la the film *American Graffiti*, while the law persons are having a coffee break.

Another tactic involves the use of the pay telephone. Call the parents of kids who get into trouble and threaten the hell out of them and their kids. You will identify yourself as Officer Hitler, or whatever name the bad cop goes by.

You could have the officer call women late at night. Call both single and married women. Sound drunk, play the radio as if the officer is in a bar. Tell the woman you saw her, fell in love, and used official records to find out her name and telephone number. Tell her you are a far better lover than she's ever had. Get graphic. Praise her anatomy specifically. Be boastful. Make demands. Make officially backed demands. If someone else, like a husband, lover, or friend, comes on the line, be abusive and drunkenly threatening. This works best if you happen to know that the cop is drinking in a local bar as you make the few calls. You might mention the name of the bar. This trick does not have to be limited to cops, but it works better that way.

Natural Gas

In previous books, I described hilarious things one can do with natural gas or to natural gas utility companies. Here's how to make your own natural gas odor solution. Ethyl mercaptan gives off an excellent natural gas odor, and it's available from chemical supply houses. One reader used it already, as Ollie Lincoln reports.

"The damn gas company kept me awake all night for three months as they drilled a well in my neighbor's field. He hated it too, but the company held the mineral and gas lease. I got some ethyl mercaptan from a chemical salesman and hit at random around the county over a few nights. I found that an ounce of it placed strategically on or near someone's home or apartment, followed by a warning telephone call, will result in a helluva lot of nasty emergency calls to that gas company in the middle of the night. It was great fun," Lincoln related.

Professor Clothespin of Boulder, Colorado tells of a revenge scam with a natural gas angle. It seems that the Professor had a pal who was seriously duped by an oily, incompetent plumber. The plumber cost this guy several thousand dollars worth of rare Persian carpets one day when a supposedly "repaired" sewer line ruptured due to the plumber's negligence. When the Professor's friend sued this swine, the case was thrown out of court, thanks to some fine print in the plumber's contract.

Here's how the Prof's buddy got even. He arranged for a crazy friend to dress up in a secondhand uniform from the local natural gas company. He even put on a real gas mask he picked up at an army surplus store. Then, at around two in the morning, he went to the mark's house carrying one of those big tool boxes. When the plumber answered the door, the disguised man waved hysterically, shouting orders to evacuate due to a bad leak. "The whole block is gonna blow!" he screamed. The plumber and his family scrammed, of course.

Into the house ran the revenge specialist. He made a hasty tour of each bathroom in the house, filling each commode with quick-setting cement he carried in his tool box. He also threw in some rotten chicken livers and old carp guts. Then he split via the back door.

The Professor reports that the mark was forced to replace every toilet in the house. The fish and chicken innards just added to the fun when the plumber started breaking up the concrete the next morning.

In this case, I'd say the punishment probably stunk more than the crime.

Neighbors

At one time in his varied occupational career, Stoney Dale had a very gossipy neighbor he called Nosey Rosey. She used to sit on the steps outside her apartment to watch which tenants came in at what time, with whom, and in what condition. Stoney says she was a "most unpleasant old gossip who made everyone miserable with her pettiness and nosiness."

Stoney noted what times she sat, and shortly before she went on her salacious sentry duty, he saturated her staircase perch with charcoal lighter fluid. Within seconds the carpeted step where Nosey Rosey always sat appeared to be high and dry. However, when the old battle-ax took her accustomed seat, her body weight caused the fluid to penetrate and soak her posterior and the light summer dress covering it. She didn't feel it until one of the other tenants called the huge stain to her attention when she arose to let him pass. She was mortified, Stoney reports, but it took two more applications to get his point across. After that, Nosey Rosey retired to her own affairs.

Who says our Canadian friends lack a sense of humor, eh? A good fan from British Columbia sent along a newspaper cutting showing how someone Hayduked his neighbor by putting a nasty sign in his yard while the property owner was on holiday. The sign read "New Satanic Church" and went on to explain in detail the doctrine of the "church." On the lawn, the Hayduker had placed a store mannequin in a black shroud and hung a dead chicken on the house. The trickster also put a sign on the front door which read, "Closed Due To Persecution." A large totem was erected with a grinning skull at the top. The entire incident was blown totally out of control by local newspaper and TV media people, much to the chagrin of the property owner who wanted it all forgotten.

Damn smart, our Canadian colleague.

If your enemy neighbor is fleeing to another town and you get his new address, keep up the action. Print a friendly invitation asking one and all of the new neighbors to the mark's new home for an introductory friendship session. You may use as your mark's theme such tie-ins as the KKK, a pro-pederasty coalition, the Communist party, American Nazi Party, et cetera. Send a copy to each neighbor. Also include nearby churches on your mailing list and post notices in neighborhood taverns and markets.

Add another to the long list of what to do when the neighbor's dog messes on you, your family, your sanity, or your property. Wilson R. Drew suggests placement of very fresh dog manure, chicken droppings, or some other odorous substance right next to the intake vent of the mark's running air conditioner. Very few marks check the conditioner, he says, so you get a lasting effect.

A little garbage goes a long way when you're trying to have as many of the other neighbors as possible hate your mark. Herb Bobwander has a beefy way to grease the trap for your mark. When he wants to do a garbage number on the mark, he takes advantage of the fact that most people put out their refuse the night before it's to be picked up.

Herb tells you to smear a lot of hamburger or bacon grease on the mark's garbage can. This will attract every animal—both wild and domestic—for blocks around, resulting in a great deal of noise, fighting, and confusion. All of this will irritate the neighborhood which will blame the mark.

After that scam bores you, take the mark's garbage can down the block and dump it in someone else's yard, or in the bed of someone's pickup truck. Or if there is an open car door, dump it in there. Or, according to Herb, you can dump it in someone's swimming pool. In all cases, someone will find a letter with an address, so your good old mark's in trouble.

As a little refinement, Herb suggests you might want to add some goodies of your own to the mark's personal garbage, e.g., sex toys, bondage magazines, gay letters, fetish things, antireligious materials, et cetera.

They surely know how to be neighborly in Northern Ireland. One such lad, a fine Irish Prossie, actually, passes along this splendid little vignette of neighborliness. It seems his American friend Tom was building his home in a rural area of Oklahoma, near the small town of Goat Testicle. His neighbor-to-be had regressed from the cross-breeding of cretins and Barbary apes. What's worse, he had a teenaged punker son. One morning, Tom looked out the window of his new home and spotted his car up on blocks with all four custom-designed mag wheels gone.

Naturally, Tom found the missing wheels had magically rolled right onto punker son's own car. Neighbor and son were, of course, wired into that incestuous Oklahoma Good Ole Boy circuit . . . you know . . . the ones who think the Jukes and Snopes are high society intellectuals. Tom knew better than to try anything official.

Tom also knew which drinking club the punker son and his father frequented. One evening, he followed them there. Waiting until they entered the establishment and settled in, Tom built a small dam of plastic under the gasoline tank of the pitiful progeny's car, then punched a tiny pinhole in the tank. He placed a glowing cigarette at the crest of the dam and ran to his own car.

"I got a bit less than a mile away when it went up—WHOOOM—most colorful and noisy. Later, I learned that the little peckerhead's car was totally destroyed," Tom said.

He added, "As an afterthought refinement, I think I would

have taken my four tires off first. Oh well . . . . "

From the epilogue standpoint, Tom says the area Good Ole Boys apparently accepted the revenge as a fortune of war. No one bothered Tom or his property again.

Suppose your hated neighbor/mark leaves his castle for a few days. You can try one of Bob Grain's stunts. He helps out by rolling up newspapers and tossing them around the front door area. He leaves notes on the door to bogus visitors about the owner being away. He cuts the main power off to make the home look more inviting to burglars as this shuts down the alarm system and the clock-controlled automatic lighting. It also has the bonus of cutting off the man's freezer. Hopefully, Bob says, a burglar will see all this and not let your efforts go to waste. Then, as Bob notes, the SOB will get ripped off. Phew!

The Midwest's famed T-Shirt Lady really poured it on when the nasty neighbors messed up her front lawn. These nasty neighbors let their downspout drain its cascades of runoff right through the T-Shirt Lady's front lawn. Not that she was a lawn 'n' grass freak or anything, but she also didn't want a duplicate of the Grand Canyon in her yard, either. After some friendly talk, requests, and other rhetorical devices brought nothing but a continued deepening of Runoff Canyon, she decided that neighborly niceness had all but eroded.

"I waited until the next really heavy downpour. Then, armed with a bit of downspout extension and a couple elbows, I quickly rerouted their drainpipe's firing path from my lawn right into their basement window."

Notary Seals

Our ideas for buying, stealing, borrowing, or otherwise obtaining a notary seal brought in some ideas on simple, inexpensive ways to create a very passable bogus item. Nasty Ned tells me he simply placed a silver dollar tails up on a stool. Then he placed the document over the coin and stood on the coin/document with a clean, rubber-heeled shoe. Naturally this "notarized" document won't stand close inspection, but how often have you ever seen any American official pay that close attention to "notarized" documents? Nasty Ned has used the tactic many times and says it works for him.

Nurses

A friend of Mark Lochte recently graduated from USC. As part of his major, he was required to pass a physical examination at the university health center. He had already had a run-in with the crabby nurse there who was more pain than a broken eyeball. He came prepared for the urinalysis part of the checkup by secreting a small can of apple juice in his pocket. Nurse Fuhrer handed him a specimen cup, aimed him at the bathroom, and commanded him to "fill."

"My friend went into the room and poured the cup half full of apple juice. He brought this out to her with a sheepish grin. She snapped at him, 'I said fill it full, bucko. Now get back in there and fill up that cup!' He shrugged, took back the cup and proceeded to drink the apple juice, then headed for the bathroom. The nurse nearly fainted," Mark relates.

Occult

Tiring of Jesus Junkies and other recruiters for the cross fouling his foyer, Barclay Mellon considered the occult as a deterrent. He eventually used other Hayduking measures to rid himself of the praying pestilence but recalled the occult when time came to teach a lesson to a pompous, nosy newcomer who was paying more than a passing fancy to Barclay's young wife.

"We lived in a Bible Belt area where people really took their devils seriously," Barclay told me. "I got a real live occultist from upstate to help me—he was only too glad to get involved. Between us, we had my region believing that the amorous newcomer was also the real live thing . . . a true disciple of the devil. It was easy: a few advertisements in the local weekly, some handbills, the endorsement of the real occultist, and a lot of rumors at local bars."

Oil Companies

A chuckle-humored Georgia reader sent his favorite oil company a delightfully devised letter, which he was willing to share with us. Dan Streetman says of his letter, "I can only gleefully imagine the havoc and expense visited upon the accounting department when this letter is handed down from the top." Here is the letter.

Dear *(Chairman of the Board);*

This is the tenth anniversary of my association with _____ Oil, and I would like to take this opportunity to thank you personally for your corporation's unflagging generosity.

It started, I suppose, with my credit application which was promptly denied for reasons I've long since forgotton. Then, strangely enough, a charge card from your company bearing my name followed shortly thereafter.

I began to use the new card routinely, assuming your credit department simply made an error in rejecting my application. I might add I used the card exclusively as I had no other gas and oil card. Two, three, four months passed; then one day it occured to me that I had received no bill. Not one. Though I kept few receipts I calculated my charges to be well over a hundred dollars at the time. As the expiration date stamped on the card approached I was certain the computer accounting error would be revealed, a mammoth bill would be sent, and no replacement card issued.

The years have clipped by now, as I've said, ten in all, and as regular as the seasons a colorful new plastic card arrives just in time to replace the old one; but never an invoice.

As gasoline prices have risen so drastically in the last couple of years I have been forced to spread your generosity by sharing my credit privileges with my friends who have found their budgets shorted by ever rising fuel costs.

This morning I had a new set of your finest line tires installed on my car. This afternoon for his birthday I am giving my friend Bob a tune-up and a brake job at another of your many, many stations. He, too, sends his best wishes for your continued success. After all these years I have grown confident that my name and number are locked, eternally silent, in a minuscule electrical impulse somewhere in some computer's faulty diode, or transistor, or senile memory bank.

Or, it may simply be that I have a secret friend or philosophical admirer in your company itself—someone who is helping me, unbeknownst to me. I wonder how many other folks are being "helped" this way and have chosen not to write you?

Unable to repay you now even if I were billed, I can only send you this note of teeming thanks.

Sincerely,

A Very Satisfied Customer

Don't you just love that dash of paranoia-producer sprinkled in at the end of the next to last paragraph? Actually, with variation and modification this letter can be used for any large credit card operation or for most utility companies. A little imagination plus some adaption will give you a custom letter to pay back some corporate tormentor, too.

Paint

Among your marks, you will find a paint freak, someone who is always touching up his house, car, fence, kids, et cetera with paint. Simply slip some luminescent paint into his bucket or sprayer. Whatever he covers with the concoction will show up eerie as hell at night.

Copper paint is a very effective addition for dressing up electrical circuits. Several readers suggested painting a thin line of copper paint down the insulator of a spark plug, for instance, running from metal to metal. If you do it on only one plug out of four, you can create electrical havoc for a mark's car by disrupting the normal circuit flow. The best part is that 99 out of 100 mechanics will never spot it as the problem . . . and all the while their $$$$ service meter is running.

Parking Tickets

If your mark gets a lot of parking tickets, here's a little extra refinement you might want to use on him or her. Remove the ticket from the car before the mark sees it. Use one of those novelty rubber stamps that features an upraised middle finger to stamp a message on the ticket, then return the mark's ticket to the police. If you don't have such a stamp, then print or type some foul message insulting to police on the ticket. Or draw something on it. Blow your nose on it. Or glue an obscene or other appropriate piece of artwork to the ticket before sending it back. Never include any money, of course.

Parties

Most of us like parties, unless they happen to be right next to where we're trying to sleep, study, read, or whatever. One Baltimore couple put up with people in the next apartment who not only didn't invite them to their blasts, but also made them suffer through the horrendously noisy debacles all evening long, then well into the morning.

"It was all screaming, singing, cursing, and the sound of things breaking and crashing," an anguished Mr. Nice-Guy-Nextdoor told me on a talk show. "The next time it happened we went over that afternoon with some coffee and light food and tried to be nice about the whole thing. They treated us like jerks.

"Their next party followed that same awful script. Only this time I got my tape recorder and very sensitive microphone up against the wall—a typically parchment-thin apartment wall—and recorded about ninety minutes of the hysteria and hoopla. They finally quit about five in the morning. At nine, I put both our huge stereo speakers right smack up against the wall where I knew their bedroom was and turned up the volume on my set as I played back their party to them.

"It took about ten minutes for that anguished couple next door to come over pleading. I smiled and said, 'Hey, I thought you were having such a good time you'd like to enjoy your party all over again.'"

It worked.

Pen Pals

Men are fools when it comes to being conned by the game that preceded even prostitution. For example, if you could create a fictional lady, she could be as seductive as you wanted her to be. After all, to the mark she is an image brought on by the words you put down on paper or maybe use on the telephone. You want him to become her pen pal.

As this scam progresses, you hope the emphasis will turn to personal matters. It's even more fun if the mark is married, because then he'll make a bigger ass of himself. Your fictional pen-pal lady must build a desire in the mark, by doing just what comes so naturally.

The climax is an assignation setup in an exotic city as far away as reality will allow. Setting up this sting calls for teasing creativity and all sorts of façades like flowers, hints of gifts, Frederick's of Hollywood apparel, bogus sexy Polaroids, etc.

The next to last thing you will do in this stunt is discontinue your post-office box or whatever mail-drop address you were using for his return messages. The last thing you will do is mail, call, or telegraph this final message, "Meet you at the Sin City Hotel, suite 625, tonight at 10 P.M. I'll have the tub and me all warm and wet."

Naturally, only one of you will arrive, and he'll hardly be in the mood to start without "you."

Personal

You can easily turn your mark into a fabled thief, according to former private detective Trowbridge Bannister. You need a full-face photo of your mark, plus a furtive longer shot of the type usually taken by surveillance cameras. Take these pictures and your WARNING copy to a trusted printer to get some posters made.

Bannister explains: "You make up posters warning merchants and customers to be on the lookout for the mark. Display his name and picture on the poster in a prominent location, along with the big headlines about this person's being a thief, shoplifter, or pickpocket. A small amount of copy could explain some brief history of your mark's criminal career. Make it sound realistic—don't get cute. Sign the thing by the local community's merchants association or something like that."

Bannister says the final step is for you to take these posters to various stores and carefully post them around the stores. Avoid being seen. Doing this in a large shopping mall or in a busy downtown area ensures that thousands of local citizens will get your message about the mark.

You could also use the same tactic and mark your mark as a sex offender, child molester, or worse...a pornographer.

You can write horrible "news" stories about your mark and have your printer set them in newspaper style, complete with column-length lines and, perhaps, border rules and datelines. You should make the dateline a town in which your mark formerly lived. In these bogus news stories, she/he could be the subject of almost any sort of execrable activity, such as child molesting, sexual perversion, child abuse, killing kittens, starving and beating puppies, poaching fawns, self abuse in public, and on and on.

Naturally, the more authentic you make the story, the better the scam will go when you send Xerox copies to the mark's employer, family, and friends. Have your mail postmarked from the mark's former city and include a short note from "a friend who thinks you ought to know the truth."

During World War II, the British SOE made use of a harassing substance that became known as "Who, Me?" It was later adopted by the American OSS. Essentially, it was a tube of obnoxious-smelling liquid that would be squirted onto an enemy's clothing or body during some time that would not cause alarm, such as while she or he was sleeping or bathing, or during the jostling of a crowd. Exposed to the air, the liquid immediately gave off the pungent odor of strong, fresh human feces.

The product was manufactured by Federal Laboratories near Pittsburgh under an OSS contract. It proved quite satisfactory and, as it was packaged, a user could eject one cubic centimeter of Who, Me? as a thin liquid stream at distances up to ten feet. There was little danger of self contamination if it was handled properly.

According to OSS records, two different formulas were used— a fecal odor for the European theater and a "skunky/body" odor for the Pacific theater. The research-backed reasoning is that because the Japanese often used human wastes as agricultural fertilizers, they would not be as sensitive to the odor as the Germans. Both forms were found to be "noticeably lasting for well over a day, despite frequent washings."

You probably want to know if you can buy surplus Who, Me? from your local army-navy outlet. No, but you can produce it yourself using the following formula:

    919 g. mineral white oil
     20 g. skatol
     20 g. n-butyric acid
     20 g. n-valeric acid
     20 g. n-caproic acid
      1 g. amyl mercaptan

That will produce a kilogram of the fecal-smelling liquid. You could alter the amounts to produce as much or as little as you think you'll need. If you prefer the skunky odor, here's the formula on a relative-percentage basis:

65 percent mineral white oil
10 percent butyric acid
10 percent mercaptan
15 percent alpha ionone

Another great pretender to aroma of woodpussy is 3-methyl-1-butane-thiol. It is easily obtainable in chemical supply stores and smells almost as terrible as the real thing.

If you are assertive enough to get the chemicals and mix up a batch of composition, you probably already have the applicator selected and don't need further help. If not, use this as a lesson in becoming more self-sufficient. Happy squirting.

If you're too insecure to become a home chemist, you could obtain some formaldehyde, which is popularly known as embalming fluid. This stuff is bad news. It stinks and can burn your skin. According to some folks, if enough of it gets into the air it will vaporize. If this takes place in a room, that room will be cleared of all breathing objects for several hours.

Being a liquid, formaldehyde may be squirted from any appropriate applicator. It is fairly devastating stuff, but you can get it in small amounts if you are involved in biological or chemical experiments. Sometimes, a white lab coat makes a good cover when you go shopping in a drugstore or medical-supply house outside your neighborhood or town.

A bit more personal, but nowhere near as dangerous, is to dip your fingers in warm water, come up behind your mark, and as you deliver an ear-shattering sneeze, fling the water on the mark's neck or back. This works well with backless dresses, at the pool, or almost anywhere, for that matter. Escape may be a vital concern here, depending on your mark's sense of humor.

If your mark is one or both members of a young couple, Dana Bearpaw had a policy of calling the parents of one or both. Playing the role of an older, irate neighbor, he would shout, "Look, I don't care how much [description of carnal activity to be left up to the discretion of the caller] your son/daughter engages in with every male/female/whatever every damn night. Just keep them out of our backyard when they're doing it. If you're any kind of a parent you'll talk to them about all this."

Parents usually take this sort of thing to heart…which causes all sorts of communication and credibility problems with their youngsters.

If you want to endear your mark to his/her neighbors, go to the local public library and consult the street-address or cross-reference city directory to learn who your mark's neighbors are and their phone numbers. If you can't find such a directory in a more rural area, just drive and list names from mailboxes.

Later, call some selected neighbors using your mark's name and be sure you identify yourself as a close neighbor. Then, launch into something like, "I want to come over and talk to you about [Communism, homosexuality, child pornography, drug legalization, busing, or whatever]. I want you to sign a petition demanding fair treatment under the law for [whatever topic you've chosen].

Be pushy and really work to make your mark's reputation a deserved one.

Many times women are certain their men are out somewhere adding significantly to the statistical rate for sexual infidelity. When one lady had absolute proof of her man's bombastic bedding habits with other ladies, she devised a scheme that would guarantee his sticking around. On one rare night when he was in their bed, his mate waited until he had fallen into his usual deep sleep, then gently applied one of the new superglue products to both his penis and his leg and held the two together for the short bonding time so well advertised on television.

No elephant, tractor, or pro footballer could break that bond. It took the delicate skill of the family physician to make the separation, a move matched that afternoon by the vindicated lady, who also cut out on her very sore ex-man.

Photography

Ask any competent photographer who also has some sense of humor, about composite photographs. They're easy to make—the tabloids used them for years. It's a photo where someone has been added to a group, someone's face has been used on the body of another person, or an entirely new photograph is created simply by using composite parts.

This is a very useful dirty trick and one that bears the stamp of approval of the CIA and the FBI.

Unless you're competent in photography, including copying, darkroom technique, and minor retouching and airbrushing, or unless you have a very trusted friend who will help you, you'd best forget this one. However, done well, the uses of composites are limited only by your imagination. Here are some examples passed along by some of the sources of this book:

- A "photo" showing the mark leaving a motel room with a person of the opposite sex.
- A "photo" sent anonymously to the police showing the mark or the mark's vehicle engaged in some illegal activity—like poaching, dealing drugs, or corrupting the morals of minors. Be sure the license number of the vehicle is visible.
- A "photo" showing the mark's spouse nude and in a compromising pose with a companion—human, animal, or whatever.

- A "photo" showing the mark in a compromising situation with a person of the same sex could be sent to the mark's employer. This will surely mark your mark a gay who will live in infamy.

Like other topical areas in this book, this one is strictly a technical suggestion. You will have to furnish the motive, rationale, and application for your own photographic nastiness.

Pilots

As a former pilot, I am used to all sorts of stories involving our airborne brethren. I once had another pilot take a dear lady friend of mine along on a trip. He put a bunch of very ungallant moves on her, culminating in a variation of the old "put out or get out" line. Not wanting to join the Mile High Club with him, she declined, and when they landed, she refused to return with this airborne asshole. Instead, she called me and asked me to come get her. Being a good buddy, I did so. I also got revenge for her.

A few weeks later, after the Philandering Pilot had forgotten the incident, I called the FAA Flight Service and filed a Visual Flight Rules (VFR) flight plan for him, using his aircraft numbers. He was on another, unfiled, flight at the time. Then I opened his "bogus" plan. However, an hour later, from an uncontrolled field where security was lax, I called the Flight Service by telephone pretending to be the mark's radio contact and announced that his radios were down and "he" was having a bit of trouble. Then I forgot about it and walked away.

When the FAA effluvia hit the prop wash, the mark—our would-be aircraft Romeo—got his tail chewed, a large bill for a false search and rescue operation, and a warning that one more even minor stunt would cost him his pilot's license. All this had a very calming effect on the man. We probably made him a better person.

Police

The late Hugh Troy mentioned earlier was a king of practical jokers. Once he had a run-in with a New York police officer in a park. The public servant was most unservile, treating Mr. Troy in a surly fashion. The next day, Hugh Troy went to the City of New York Office of Property and Supply and bought a park bench for a good deal of money. He had it delivered to the same park where the officer had accosted him. He and two friends did this before the cop's beat began. As soon as they saw the cop approaching, they picked up the bench and started away with it.

To keep this story short, they told the cop they were simply taking the bench home. They did nothing to resist arrest and didn't show anyone any sales papers, or tell anyone about the purchase until their preliminary hearing. The furious judge asked Hugh Troy why he hadn't told the beat cop about buying the bench. Mr. Troy replied that the officer (a) had never asked him, and (b) told him he didn't want to hear a peep out of him. The judge gave the cop hell right in front of everyone and released Hugh Troy and friends. So much for bench-pressed justice.

Why don't people respect our police? Detroit Jerald tells me this true story of what's been going on for years now in the American automobile industry. It seems when the car companies make a run of police cruisers, word rolls down the line, and many workers break out supplies of food waste, garbage, roadkill, and so on, which they hide in the cruisers at various stages of construction. Supervisors and checkers often look the other way. Car 54, what's happened to you?

Politicians

You can build a photographic frame around the candidate of your dischoice. Suppose one of these slugs displeases you more than others, for any number of valid reasons. You need some scuzzy friends to pull this one off. You wear a T-shirt with a militant slogan at extreme odds with the politician, e.g. POLITICIANS ARE INEVITABLY IDIOTS. But, you have it disguised under something, like a book bag or by holding a newspaper in front of yourself. Your odd friends cluster behind the politician.

This works best at campaign time when there are a lot of cameras around. You come up to the politico/mark with your hand extended for the usual shake. Your partners move into position—clustered around the two of you. As you and the mark shake hands this is what will appear in the photo:

- You reveal your messaged T-shirt.
- One of your pals behind the mark gives the raised/clenched fist salute.
- Several of your pals hug and pretend to french kiss each other, as in a gaggle of gays.
- Another of your pals exposes himself.
- Another produces a bottle in a brown bag.
- And, so on. . . .

If your photos turn out you have that candidate by his or her photogenic short hairs.

Porno

Yes, porno theaters can cause problems in a neighborhood simply because of some of the pathetic slimes who are drawn there like slugs to a wet garden. Or, you can be ripped off by a porno theater that promises you a loop done by Brooke Shields in her early years, showing her wrestling naked with, well, you fill in your favorite fantasy. But, it's merely a raunchy lookalike. Sigh. You're out $10.

How to get even?

Dress up like some pimpy businessperson, slick back your hair, then buy a ticket and go into the theater. Once inside, start handing out free passes you had printed just for this occasion.

The passes are a special invitation to see a commercially produced snuff film, with a real on-camera homicide. If you want to go to the trouble and expense, print a little brochure with obscene photos and maybe a composite showing some sexual and/or violent action. You can probably get pictures of this garbage from militant feminist groups who want to publicize the degradation of obscene films. Put the address of the porno theater (your mark) on the brochure along with a time and date. Work quickly and get out of there as soon as possible.

As an additional fun thing, on the day of the "showing," be certain to get these same passes and brochure to local media people, clergy, feminist groups, local redneck politicans, police, etc.

Just suppose, for the sake of argument, that some fat jackass of a District Attorney or shyster lawyer for some blue-nosed Citizens for Decent Literature group wins one of their censorship cases. These lowlifes are the bookburners who piously demand that all of us follow their stupidly moral misvalues. Here's how Emmett Hillard got even when they closed down his book store in Gipsy, Missouri, because a copy of *Sports Illustrated* had a picture on its cover of a lady in a bikini.

"I found the most graphic and active swingers' magazine I could. Then, I searched up in the city for the foulest and most perverted sexual magazines published. And, in each, I placed a small display advertisement for the leader of the local Bible bangers who closed me down."

His ad read:

FREE

TALK YOUR DIRTIEST FOR ONE MINUTE

Call this number and say the dirtiest most perverted things you can think of . . . my friend and I
will outdo you. Cum again? We hope so.
Ring our dingy!!!

Name . . . Home Telephone Number

According to Hilliard, every sewer mouth from Fairlawn to Niwot, from Butler to Helsinki lathed the ears of the mark, his wife and his daughter until he finally had to have his telephone number changed . . . several times.

"The best part is that it took three months from when he did me dirty until I got back, because of publication lag and all that. It was great. I will hit him again," says Hilliard.

This next trick will work well if your mark is a spoiled brat or bratess who has not yet been cut loose from the family apron. Get a rubber stamp made that says something tacky like YE SEXY LEATHER SHOPPE, or S & M LEATHERETTES, or something else that implies kinky, gay sex involving leather,

182

freakos, S & M, etc. Apply the imprint to a cheapie type manila mailing envelope with a metal clasp on it. Fill this envelope with gay magazines, explicit brochures, S & M propaganda, etc. Then, get a lady with nice handwriting to write a note on cutesy pink paper. The note should be addressed to your mark personally and say something like, "Bunny gave us your home address, sweetcakes. He/she said you'd enjoy dreaming about our next gay ball if you had these to look at first while you fantasize about doing it with us. Keep cumming back to our parties. Love, Brucie."

Don't glue this envelope shut. Simply seal it. Then, address it to your mark and send it to his home address. Hopefully, it will create some wildly *loco parentis.*

Postal Service

M. J. Banks once sent her mother a Bible via the U.S. Postal Service. By the time it arrived, seven of the Ten Commandments were broken.

If you like your mail deliverer but dislike the U.S. Postal Service, Loren Eugene Sturgis has good news for you. He feels that ordinary citizens are already subsidizing the big corporations and their junk-mail advertising. He fights junk mail, which we'll get to in a moment. But, here is one of Loren's ways of cutting down on your own personal postal overhead.

Use Elmer's glue to coat the surface of stamps. This substance defeats the cancellation imprint enough that when you soak the stamp in lukewarm water, both the Elmer's and the cancellation ink come right off. Then you reglue the back of the stamp and use it again and again and again. This is a real money-saver for those who use a lot of postage, Loren points out. Your local postmaster would also point out how illegal this stunt is. Whom would you rather believe?

Rufus and Ruthie Luv are true rebels. Ruf used to work for the postal service, and he claims that automatic sorting machines really can't tell stamp denominations. For example, he said letters do go through with Easter Seals in place of stamps. He also suggests placing your stamp in the lower right corner. That way, the automatic canceling device will miss it and someone can reuse the stamp.

The U.S. Postal Service also furnishes you with games you can play with your mark. If you've ever moved, you know how happy USPS is to give you change-of-address cards. OK, you get such a card and change your mark's address. It would be good if you had his mail sent to another state. Don't get exotic, though; keep it simple. Use a larger city, like Los Angeles, since this increases the likelihood of further screw-ups as the mark attempts to straighten out the mess when he discovers his mail is no longer arriving. You can double the trouble by changing both home and business addresses. Stop a few moments and think how fouled up your own life would be if your mail was suddenly diverted and possibly lost. It's just a thought....

Posters

Here's one that John Bowen calls his "Tribute to Dallas." If you have an incumbent President you don't like, run off a few of the "(NAME OF PRESIDENT): WANTED FOR TREASON" posters of the type that were used in Dallas the week before President Kennedy was murdered there by some determined assassins. They used JFK's name as the traitor. Your kicker is that you put your mark's name in small type as sponsors of the poster, then list some affiliation, e.g., the Klan, the Birchers, the Nazis, the U.S. Labor Party, etc., under his name. Obviously, this can be used at most any level of policies.

There are also political endorsement modifications available on this one. Think of all the fun you can have with gay rights groups, pro-life, or pro-abortion people who could have their "names" listed on the posters you're having printed.

Projectiles

A thin-shelled paint grenade can be made using the basics of that old childhood game of pinholing the two ends of an egg, then blowing out the gloop. Use a needle and syringe to fill the empty shell with colorful, permanent drawing ink. Close with glue, locate your mark, then color to distraction. This bit of artistic application comes from Alan Kuenau, another California follower of the Order of St. Hayduke.

PA Systems

Almost all large department stores and mall shops have employee and PA phones all over the store. Try to identify the main PA system line button, then locate an isolated station where you can use that phone unobserved. Compose the most objectionable statement you can imagine that you can deliver in about five seconds. Make it gross, sick, insulting, or obscene (best if you can combine all of them). Write it down. Then read it over the store's PA line. Hang up the phone and walk briskly away. Look as shocked as the rest of the customers in the store who heard your message. Do it again another day or at random intervals. Always end by saying, "This message brought to you by the management of (*store name*)."

Railroads

If a railroad line has been nasty to you and you want to get back, you are welcome to follow "Bart's" advice. A fan of Edward Abbey, "Bart" offers you the following from his trickster's arsenal. Set the manual brakes on railroad cars; this will cause a great deal of delay in checking and rechecking, which ties up people, time, and money. You can visit the railyard areas on cold, cold nights in winter and pour lots of water on the switch points. This freezes the switches, making them inoperable.

Religion

This one's pretty rough and if you have a streak of old-fashioned religion in you, perhaps you'd best skip this section. The Rev. Sam Clayton Neucomber split with traditional religion some years ago and now fights the IRS and other establishment evils from his own parish in Arizona.

He says, "It's not enough to merely corrupt the mark's religious beliefs or to start rumors about him or her in the church. You have to do more, expecially if your mark is a church or a movement."

If your mark is a house of worship or the wordly master of that house, e.g., the religious person in charge, the good Rev. Neucomber has some interesting ideas.

"It's not nearly enough just to insult or mock a religious mark," says Rev. Neucomber. "You must go beyond the mere passion of punks or vandals. To really flip out your mark you must create a scene that leaves no doubt the religious shrine or church or whatever was broken into for the express purpose of holding a Black Mass, for example.

"The mark will call out to God, asking what manner of devil or demented heathen would desecrate His house of worship in such a way. Here's where imagination comes in well."

Some of Rev. Neucomber's suggestions for evidence of a Black Mass include:

- Leave animal blood, unless you can get human blood in quantity, on marble areas or splashed over the altar.
- Leave an especially ghoulish animal sacrifice there too.
- If there is a table cloth there, perhaps for communion services, you can adorn it with occult symbols and bestial graffiti.
- Scatter photos around which show naked women blindfolded, bound and gagged. Make sure some of the photos show the women in sexually open and totally vulnerable positions. Child porn would work here, too.
- Mutilate some of these photos, marking them with blood and symbolically destroying genital areas.
- Leave used condoms around—some filled with semen, others with blood.
- Use some of the mark's fine chalices and leave a few filled with urine. Pour blood in a couple and be sure at least one has semen in it.

Phew . . . if you're still with us, did you ever work with a religious hot dog, the type who overtries to convert everyone else in the place? Dingo L. Stuart had to put up with one of these yoyo's during his tour of duty working in a large factory. Tiring of the Bible banger's shrieks and tirades, Stuart called on his pal, who worked in a print shop.

Together, they come up with sophisticated looking ecclesiastical stationery on which they printed CERTIFICATE OF EXORCISM in an old fashioned churchy-appearing type style. The document stated, "In a Secret Ceremony witnessed by (name all sorts of angels, martyrs, deceased heroes, etc.) the Reverend (Use name of some other mark) did hereby and forever expel and exorcize the unclean spirits from the body and soul of (Name of your main mark here), releasing him from the torments of everlasting hell and damnation. (Name of main mark)'s soul will now ascend to His Paradise."

Feel free to edit or rewrite that as you wish, customizing it for your mark. Stuart says to include with this statement an itemized fee schedule for the Exorcism, including the cleric's fee, costs for candles, incense, bottled blood, vestments which had to be burned, a sacrificial calf or goat—use your imagination. Total it, then send the entire thing to the mark's supervisor, along with a bogus cover letter on the same letterhead asking the employer's help in dunning the employee who has not paid for the exorcism.

As a possible alternative plan, you could simply send a letter on that letterhead to the supervisor, from the Reverend, saying that the main mark, the religious nut employee, had suggested his name (the employer or supervisor) as being in need of salvation, or even an exorcism, too. Include a copy of that exorcism statement mentioned earlier.

Restaurants

It used to be annoying when a waitress accidentally stuck her thumb in your soup while serving you lunch. That was before topless waitresses, however.

Suppose you're really fried with a local eatery for charging you for terrible food time after time, and are ready to wash your hands of the whole place. Try silver nitrate instead. If you can introduce a bit of that chemical into the soap dispenser in the restaurant washroom, you will have customers and employees furious with the restaurant. Silver nitrate will leave their hands and faces unwashably stained to an ugly, erratic brown color. It does not come off easily.

Harry Katz, a prominent Pennsylvania socialite, frequents many posh dining establishments in the company of equally ritzy jet setters. He insists that this scam is only a practical joke, which may be correct. However, with a bit of malice aforethought, someone could easily create a nasty version. Harry carries with him a supply of elegantly printed cards. He spots someone he wishes to hassle and bribes a waiter to carry one of the cards over to the mark. The card reads, "The management requests that you and your party leave immediately before we have to call the authorities."

Of course, we don't always have to be so sophisticated. If there are entire groups of people you don't like, you can always eat in restaurants frequented by such people and put salt into the sugar dispensers or unscrew the tops of the salt and pepper shakers, so that the next diner gets a plate full of seasoning. Of course, such stunts are perilously close to April Fool amateurism, but they do have some minor harassment value.

If you had a friend who would take care of the tab, you'd take that friend out to dinner, right? In some swanky and excellent eatery, order your finest repast. Treat yourself to the best. About halfway through the meal, you introduce that friend who's going to take care of your tab. Your friend is a dead cockroach that you brought in with you, carried carefully in your jacket pocket. Place your late friend amid some food on your plate and then turn on your theatrics. Make a noisy fuss and express concern about your health and the restaurant's cleanliness standards, and mutter about your lawyer filing an action. After this, let the management talk you into a free meal or two and some drinks.

This next trick will costs a few bucks, but if you consider it as a perverted investment, the return will be worth many times the outlay. For example, a small display ad could be run in either a campus newspaper or one of the small local newspapers or shoppers. Pick one that isn't too professional, since they are less likely to check the veracity of the ad.

The ad promises some fantastic dinner bargain, such as a steak dinner for two at half price, when the clipped ad is presented between 6 and 7 o'clock that night. Or promise an All You Can Eat Special of roast steamship round of beef for three dollars, with all the trimmings, also with the clipped ad. Use the logo of the restaurant with which you are feuding in the ad. Check their regular ads so your layout looks authentic. Take it in and tell them you're the new assistant who handles advertising. Just don't spend too much time talking or getting remembered. Be prepared to pay cash if necessary.

Between 6 and 7 P.M. your mark will literally have his restaurant crammed with very hungry and soon-to-be-very-unhappy customers. By 8 P.M. the owner could have a whole lot of ex-customers and an undeserved bad reputation that will be hard to overcome. Or the owner may decide to go along with the "promise," which will cost her/him a lot of bucks. Finally, there will be an unpleasant scene with the newspaper. This scam will also work with local radio stations.

Note, too, that this scam can be turned so that the mark is the newspaper or radio station.

Return Envelopes

Always salvage business reply envelopes you receive in the mail from institutions, businesses, government agencies, et cetera. Especially good are envelopes that were not sealed well or that you opened without tearing. Or if you can get a supply when you are visiting an office, keep that in mind, too. These make great containers for sending materials to your mark, as they identify a second mark for the first mark to puzzle over as he or she ponders "why me" in reference to the contents of your parcel.

Roadkill

There are always rednecks who love to destroy animals who venture out on our interventionist highways. I remember almost dismembering some illiterate jackass who was driving an UPS truck down the lane to my old home fortress a few months back. He was proud that he'd run over a blacksnack on my lane. He told me so. I was not thrilled and told him that that specific snake kept little varmints out of my garden. His sloped brow sunk lower, then he told me that he read in the *National Enquirer* that blacksnakes and rattlesnakes were mating, causing a new breed of poisonous snake. I told him I wished his parents had heard of birth control, but probably not so much as they did now, like every time they saw him. He took a swing at me five minutes later, when what I said sunk through the bone. He later threatened to sue me for the damages he then picked up. Later, calling him at home, I told him he'd better watch out for his mailbox as I had friends in Synanon who trained rattlesnakes.

Whatever, I researched his route and talked to people who lived along it. I learned he would swerve to scare dogs playing along the road. One old soul told me that this UPS driver seemed to have a thing for running over animals on purpose.

Thanks to some help from a friend of a friend of a friend at the SPCA, I found a dog that had been freshly killed by a passing car. I had that friend claim the carcass and get it to me. I armed it with some low grade explosives, wired it with a very simple pressure detonator that you can duplicate by reading a specific military demolition manual, then laid it along the route taken by my UPS mark.

Sure enough, numbnuts tried to squash the already dead dog one more time. The ordnance did its thing and his company vehicle was minus one tire, had another one flattened, there was minor structural damage, while our driver was a total nervous wreck. It took him one week to get physically together and three more weeks before he could get into another truck. The best is that UPS and his union disciplined him for reckless operation.

Rock Stars

Want to create a riot in your town? Want to make the life of a record, music, or video store manager miserable? Advertise that a cult rock or film star will make a nonscheduled appearance at the mark's store. You have no idea what sort of damage will be caused by a few hundred hardcore fans when their idol doesn't show up and the ugly word "hoax" goes through the crowd. Maybe you could be there to spread the word.

Roofs

Windy City Pat told me about a roofing company that contracted to do his home and not only overcharged him, but didn't do their job properly either. It took all sorts of threats to get them to make things right. It took so much grief and hassle out of Pat that he decided to do something about it.

Pat recalls, "I talked with a friend of mine who was a city building inspector, and he told me an old roofer's dirty trick. Toss a couple bars of plain soap into the tar bath used by the roofing company (Pat's mark). I did this unobserved during a lunch break, hitting all three baths they had going on a large industrial project. It made the tar bubble over in all the wrong places, took them three days to clean up their mess, and some money to settle some potential lawsuits for the spillage."

Rotten Egg Smells

When I first heard this one, it brought back memories of mass menu recipes I ran into when I was Uncle Sam's guest. You know, 195 gallons of this, eighty-six pounds of that, sixty-one carcasses of these, several bales of whatizit, and so on. Anyway, this is a recipe for making a massive quantity of a solution that, according to its chief cook, smells *worse* than terminally rotten eggs.

The Rev. J. Richard Young is our mass-amount chef, and here's his recipe: Boil twenty-five pounds of sulfur in a fifty-five gallon drum over a hot fire, adding fifty pounds of lime and water. After hard boiling for an hour, kill the fire and let the mixture sit overnight to cool. Carefully siphon off the yellowish/orange liquid, but leave the settled lime and sulphur. Fill the drum with water, stir the mixture, and bring it to a boil again. Let it settle and cool for another night, and again pour off the liquid.

According to the good reverend, you should now have about thirty to forty gallons of stock. To this, add one pound of sulphate of ammonia fertilizer for each gallon of liquid you have. Stir it, and then cover the mixture. After an hour or so, it will stink awesomely, and you are advised to cover it tightly. To quote one witness who attended its use once in Winslow, Arizona, the afflicted area smelled "worse than if every sewer in town had backed up fully in the middle of summer . . . It was sickenly gross."

Rubbers

Here's a quickie that can annoy your mark, if you have easy access to his boots, overshoes or rubbers on a winter or rainy day. If you know when he or she is going to be putting them on, pour some slow drying glue into the footwear a bit before they go on the mark's shoes. Spread the stuff around so it bonds well.

Snowmen

You remember back in your days of innocence when you'd see little kids building snowmen during our old-fashioned and benign winters? The tykes would work all afternoon perfecting their masterpiece. That evening, lowlife older kids would come by and kick it and tackle it, bashing it down. Or older derelicts would drive their cars into the little kids' snowmen, destroying everything.

Consider, though, what would happen if these little kids got some advice and help so that they built their snowperson around a fire hydrant, a cement pole, a tree stump, or something else that would give a person or a car equal or worse impact damage.

Sperm Banks

This slippery little trick ought to get up the dander of most people. So we owe a special thank you to a good friend, Dr. Wilbur Nosegay. To start this one, you need to make some Xerox machine letterhead that says something like: "Reproduction Researchers" or "Sperm Donors Anonymous."

The operation begins when you use this letterhead to prepare a solicitation letter to your mark, enclosing a vial or tube with the letter. Tell the mark you are paying ten dollars for a shot of his sperm. Enclose a medical form for him to fill out noting name, age, date, IQ, race, and time of emission. This one is perfect for multi-mark use, too.

If, God forbid, any mark is stupid enough to comply and you should somehow get the vials returned to a real post office box (this is all in theory, of course), you can simply remail them to the mark's girlfriend, wife, mother, minister, et cetera. In reality, it is best not to use your real post office box on your return address. If you're smart, that box number will belong to some secondary mark.

Supermarkets

In addition to switching labels on food cans, described
elsewhere in this work, one of my disciples suggests buying the
new pump bottles of such things as furniture and car polish,
taking them home, then replacing the original contents with
harmful acids and corrosive contents. Next, smuggle them back
into the store, or directly into your mark's home if possible,
depending on who or what your mark is. Hee Hee, watch the
mark really get red and raw hands from the old chores . . . not to
mention the old redass!!

Sweepstakes

The reason that con artists succeed is that people are basically greedy and sometimes a bit dishonest, e.g., most folks want something for nothing, and all of us are bargain hunters. That's what Casey Rolands of Tampa, Florida had in mind when he shared this scam.

"All you do is call thirty or forty people in your city and read a written statement which you present after making them identify themselves. You tell each person something along the line of 'Congratulations, (name of person called), you've won our free telephone (name some other secondary mark like a business or radio station) sweepstakes. No, this is no gimmick and not a sale. It's just our free sweepstakes to show people in (town name) how much we love 'em. To collect your prize call (then give them the mark's number) and ask for (mark's first name).' "

You may answer questions but always seem excited and urge them to call today, as Casey adds with a laugh.

"If you want to build it up a bit, identify yourself as being from some local outfit that regularly gives away huge sums of money. It works so well that irate people will call the mark for weeks wondering what happened to their prize money," he says.

Sweethearts

Did you ever notice those tabloids and semiskin flicks that run classified ads headlined "Foreign Girls Looking For American Husbands"? One young lady learned about that after her married lover ditched her because *she* made the stupid mistake of getting pregnant by him. Instead of moping, she had the good sense to get even with the subhuman slimeball. Here's how.

"I sent off a response to one of those ads, written as if a hot to go, but sincere, guy who wanted both marriage and action would write it," she told me. "I heard enough of that kind of BS from that (expletive deleted) who burned me."

What happens is that the foreign recipient will get the hot letter and she will go directly to the mark. The foreign stamp on the envelope and lady's handwriting will cause great curiosity on the part of the mark's wife. She might say, "Hmmm, we don't know anyone in the Philippines . . . do we?

The next sound you hear is an envelope being opened.

The next idea is a bit different. It started when the girl slapped Frank Fogge, gave him back his picture and told him to get lost. She had been won over by a kid with more money and status on the football team. She said she'd carry the New Sweetie's picture with her forever. She told Frank this new love was inscribed on her soul.

Fogge was no dummy, and he didn't mope around either. He

got even. He gave her another picture to think about.

Using a standard billing form available from any stationery department, Fogge prepared a bogus invoice from "Sammy's Tattoo Parlor," complete with address and a catchy business motto. He got the business logo done by instant lettering, an inexpensive commercial process, then filled in the invoice information by hand. He also got a rubber stamp that spelled OVERDUE in big letters, and put a huge red stamping of this on the invoice.

Finally, he wrote a cover letter from "Sammy," explaining to the ex-girlfriend's parents that their daughter had gotten "a tasteful facial tattoo," but, that she was now upset after a few days and was refusing to pay for it. He wrote that it would make a huge scar if it were removed, and that he just wanted to be paid. He noted, "She is your problem now, but I want my money."

On the other hand, if your mark is a newlywed, or one of those Pat Boone squares, this trick is quite nice. Your printer sets up and prints a "Preferred Customer Credit Voucher" sales gimmick. The rest of the copy informs the holder that he will get a $10 credit toward a "full body massage with complete fulfillment by our . . ." you can use your prurient imagination to fill in the nubile delights of the maiden whose hands, mouth and other goodies will delightfully satisfy the customer.

You send this card to the mark's business address in hopes his secretary will open it. Or, if your mark doesn't have a secretary, send it home. Make it personal and put perfume on it. If his blueturning, red hot wife doesn't open it, she surely as hell will demand he does, in front of her. Do you note a different type of massage or even message coming up?

A really nasty friend gave me this one. This chap is so bad he has plastered his car bumper with NUKE THE WHALES stickers, while his favorite adult toy to tinker with is a submachine gun. He's a good beer drinker and has a very nasty turn of mind. I guess that's why we're friends.

Anyway, it seems a friend of my friend got the shaft from his former girl friend who tossed him over for a richer man who was able to entertain her on a champagne budget. He wanted to get back at the snooty bitch. Happily, her father was a real racist redneck, which made it easier.

His scam went like this. Our young man got a black friend who has mastered a real Stepin Fetchit approach to the Negro dialect. The black buddy called the girl's home telephone at some ungodly hour of the early morning, knowing full well the young woman lived in her own apartment elsewhere in the city. When the sleepy parent answered, the buddy launched into his hip-black monologue, saying that Ellen was supposed to come back to his pad to pick up some personal effects she had left there last night.

According to my pal, this trick will provoke the racist, over-protective father into a state of cardiac paranoia. When it was first tried by my friend, he said it took the father 20 minutes to dress and drive across the city to rescue "his little girl" from the subhuman clutches of her imaginary Black stud. Watching the fun from a nearby room, my friend reported a terrible argument with much shouting and ranting. This wakened the neighbors, creating more fuss and furor. Eventually, the police had to be called. It was great sport, according to my friend. It sounds it to me, too.

Then, there is the story of Young Sam, who dated a coed who treated him like a visiting monk. In the meantime, she milked his jealousy by flirting with all sorts of other guys at parties. When they were alone, she kept her clothes on tighter than a professional virgin. When Sam learned her parents were coming to visit he had a plan. He acquired some suspiciously stained men's underwear of the sexy type. He made little typed plaques with the autographs of some campus studs, e.g., Black football players, etc., plus inscriptions like "To _____ , "Wow, _____ , I told you a threesome was more fun . . . love, _____ ."

While sweet young thing was out to meet her parents Sam snuck into her apartment and mounted the trophies on the wall of her bedroom. He left the rest to the imagination of her parents.

You've heard of the pregnant pause? You want to break up with your two-timing lady? Daniel Jackson has the answer. He says you should take this lady out for a fashionable meal in a very posh restaurant. Or, if you live in a small town, take her to the place where all the old gossips chow down. Whatever, after ordering the most expensive stuff on the menu, about the time the little snacks and talk food are served, stand bold-upright, look at her, then scream "PREGNANT? Pregnant, my ass! You never did that with ME!!"

Then, you slam down you napkin and stride quickly out of the place. She has to pay for both meals *and* has some explaining to do.

Not everyone is like that. There's a nice young lady who used to call herself Becky Buckeye. But, with the coming of Born Again Reagan Power, she changed her name to Becky Beaver. I'm not even going to attempt any thoughts about all that. As you'll agree, her diabolical suggestion is all the bonafides she needs in our movement.

Becky relates that a friend of hers had some man problems in that he wouldn't limit his personal charms to her.

Becky says, "She planted a birth control pill box with a few days punched and the rest missed. Now, some people might not start counting days. But, this guy would begin to mark off a mental calendar."

For those of you who are not physio-chemically inclined, Becky explains that the mark will think his lady friend was not taking her pill each day, which can easily lead to one becoming of the pregnant persuasion if other variables are also present. The point is to panic the man into thinking he is soon to become an involuntary parent.

Becky's friend says this causes all sorts of anxieties, paranoia, personality quirks and expression of true feelings. The latter is especially important. Becky also adds that if the mark doesn't have a steady woman this is far less effective as a trick on him.

Here's one Wilbur Aaron was itching to share with like-minded readers. Seems a snotty little bitch was patronizing and nasty to Wilbur Aaron's best friend when she told him their romance was over right then and there. She said coldly, "I'm itching to meet someone with more class and money. You're nothing but a weed in my social garden."

With that, she signed on as an habitué of the local singles bar meat markets in hopes of meeting true love and lust. Instead of hoping she'd meet Mr. Goodbar, Wilbur's friend thought about what she'd told him. He came up with an extremely clever use of poison ivy.

"Although it was a month or so after she tossed him out for no good reason other than her own ego, he still had a key to her place that she'd forgotton about. Thus, he had easy acces to the leotard she wore to her dance class," Wilbur reports.

The lacerated ex-lover liberally smeared the groin and chest areas inside of the leotard with crushed poison ivy. Later that day, the exertion in her dance class opened up her pores and she soon had a splendid outbreak of the virulent rash in those most sensitive areas.

"As she washed the leotard after every class she never associated it with that mysterious rash that popped up two days later. It was a dilly," Wilbur adds.

Swimming Pools

John Lutz, a libation specialist, made a delightful discovery while shopping for something actively stronger than those comedic "I DON'T SWIM IN YOUR TOILET, SO PLEASE DON'T PEE IN MY POOL" posters that do so little. He learned that a chemical substance sold by the trade name of Aquatect makes a positively great additive to your swimming pool water.

"It is odorless and colorless and cannot be detected in the pool, until a swimmer pees, then the chemical reacts with the urine and creates a bright red stain around the culprit," Lutz explains.

Tailgaters

When moldy motorheads used to drive up behind me in the typical tailgate approach, I used to slow down to fifteen MPH. But this usually inconvenienced me more than it irritated them. I was overjoyed a few years ago when I saw a bumper sticker on a car parked in a small lot near Washington. It read *Honk if You're an Asshole.*

"Perfect idea," I said aloud to myself. "All we need to do is add the word 'tailgating' before 'asshole' or 'tailgater' after it."

Another antitailgating tactic comes form Wise King Cobra who uses a two-phase toggle switch to back the bastards away from his vehicle. His first switch is hooked to his brake lights, and when some yo-yo crawls up Cobra's bumper, he hits that switch. A few flicks and some tailgaters back off. Others need more of an adrenalin boost. That's what the second switch is for. It is hooked to the Cobra's backup lights.

"It's damn tough to follow someone as close as tailgater does and not get that loose-bowel feeling when you see backup lights flare up right in front of your face. They *always* fall back after that. I've even seen some run off the road. That's a wonderful feeling."

Teachers

Early one morning before their teacher got to the classroom, some students painted a large black/brown spot on the ceiling. With some deft art touches, it looked as if a huge hole had suddenly broken through. They piled broken plaster, ceiling wire, and hunks of lath on the floor beneath the hole.

The teacher was a priss, and when he came in and saw the mess he pranced out to inform the principal. Quickly, the perpetrators cleaned the water paint off the ceiling and swept up the floor. They disposed of the residue and trash on the roof outside the room.

When the principal and the teacher returned, the students acted innocently concerned about the teacher's sanity. The principal asked the teacher to please stop in and see him at the first available moment. As he left, the principal stared at the teacher for a long, long time.

If you don't like a teacher, here's the ticket, according to that veteran student of human affairs Doug Dedge. You have to get your mark to a library where they use an electronic sensor to catch people taking books out of the place without proper checkout. Locate your mark. Then go to the periodicals section and page through magazines until you locate and remove several of the metallic sensor strips.

Carefully plant these on your mark or on his/her own books,

briefcase, overcoat, or whatever. The idea is to get multiple plantings. Perhaps a diversion could be created to allow you the few seconds needed to plant the sensors. Stick around and enjoy the fun when the mark tries to go out the door.

Your planted sensors will set off the bell. This will cause extreme shock, upset, indignation, and confusion. With luck, only one sensor will be found at first, and the mark will try to leave again. Round two is also yours.

Because teachers deal with children, they are especially susceptible to child-molesting charges, deserved or not. Claude Pendejo's son was accused by his teacher of cheating on a test and given an F. The boy, who was quite innocent, literally cried his innocence. No one believed him but his parents. The teacher was especially insolent about the entire matter, refusing to even talk with the parents. The teachers' union backed their errant member, and that caused the principal to shy away from the case.

Claude Pendejo decided that because this teacher had messed up his son, it was only fitting for the man to become a molester of a different sort.

After giving the teacher a couple of months to forget the incident, Pendejo acted. One morning, each home in the neighborhood around this school was posted with a brief letter, run off on a cheap mimeo machine. The letter stated that the teacher in question had molested the little child of the letter's grieving writer—a scared mother—and only now did this parent have the courage to come forth. The "writer" of the letter said that the teacher had sexually abused her son on four occasions, and finally the pain and shame had made him come to his parents for salvation. The "humble mother" said the police would do nothing, so she, as a frightened mother, was appealing directly to other concerned parents for their help in ridding their neighborhood school of this horrible beast.

Within three days, the man was blamed (wrongly) for an actual molesting incident totally unrelated to the scam. Two other kids came forward and "confessed" he had made sexual advances to them (he had not). The man was waylaid by two fathers and pushed around, his car was trashed, and the neighborhood cop told him he would have his eye on the man. The teacher's wife was a suspicious sort anyway, and this whole thing just fed their marital fires. Finally, his supervisor told the man he was too much of a problem and he ought to consider either moving away or going into a new line of work. This happened after the local paper ran a "guilty or no" story on the whole matter. Since there was no actual proof, the paper was somewhat sympathetic to the mark. Eventually, the whole matter burned down to a few embers of suspicion that would never die out.

Telephones

Until I considered some of my acquaintances as potential marks, I could not believe that this scam was serious, especially since the wonderful humorist H. Allen Smith suggested it. You call your mark, identify yourself as being from the telephone company's service division, and say something like this:

"We're calling to warn you that we're going to be blowing out the telephone lines this afternoon. We advise you to cover your telephone with a plastic bag, and under no circumstances should you use it between the hours of 1 and 4 P.M. If the instrument is not covered you run the risk of having the receiver damaged and of having grease and soot from the lines blown into your home should the receiver be lifted from the phone during this line-cleaning operation. Thank you, blah, blah. . . ."

Smith swore he had personal knowledge that this bit works. That's good enough for me. Have a blowing good time cleaning out someone's telephone line.

This next stunt works best early in the morning, late in the day, or always with some people. Pick out that special jerk and call him/her on the telephone. Here's how to run the conversation.

YOU: Hello, who is this please?
MR. ELDER: This is Mr. Elder.

YOU: Oh, I'm sorry—he's not here right now.

MR. ELDER: What? Who's not there?

YOU: Mr. Elder is not here.

MR. ELDER: Wait a minute, *I'm* Mr. Elder. *You* called—

YOU: [*interrupting Mr. Elder*]: I'm sorry, sir—Mr. Elder just [stepped out, is in a meeting, isn't at his desk, etc.] right now. May I have him call you back?

MR. ELDER: You fool, *I* am Mr. Elder. I didn't call him; I *am* him. You made this call. *You* called *me. I'm* Mr. Elder!

YOU: Will you please calm down, sir, and let me have your name and number. I'll have Mr. Elder call you just as soon as he gets back. Actually, he really went across the street to get [a drink, shot up with dope, laid]. We're having some really terrible problems with him.

By now the line will have gone dead. If Mr. Elder doesn't hang up, you should, after the usually cheery and phony "Have a nice day, now. You have gone a long way toward ruining Mr. Elder's day.

Starting at about 2:30 A.M., call the mark's home. When he/she answers, ask for someone, anyone ... let's say you ask for Dave Rottedgel.

"Dave who?" says the sleepy voice.

"Dave Rottedgel. Is he there?"

The mark growls, "No, you have a wrong number." About fifteen minutes later, using a different voice or having an associate call, do it again. And again. And again. Always ask for the same person—in this case, Dave Rottedgel. When the caller(s) feel the mark is starting to get really hot and has probably had his or her sleep ruined for that night, it is time for the final call.

"Hello, [use mark's first name] ?"

Wearily and probably snappishly, the mark will answer, "Yes, it is."

"Hey, this is Dave Rottedgel. Any calls for me?" The way to handle wrong numbers in a nasty way is to wait for a few moments of silent effect to build up just after you answer the phone, then laugh as hollowly and mockingly as you can right into the mouthpiece. Never utter a word. Just give 'em that horrible, hollow laugh and hang up. Don't answer the phone if it rings again shortly.

Before taking the vows, Sister Laverne Finneri, of Our Mother of Perpetual Flatulence, used to be a telephone trickster. Her best fun came in calling about two hundred people and hoping that in at least fifty cases, the asked-for party was not home but a message could be taken.

"Thank you, would you please have [name of party to get message] call [name of mark] back any time after midnight tonight. Yes, it is very, *very* important or I wouldn't ask you to have him/her call so late."

Laverne reports that it worked. "I used to check it out by calling the mark's number around 1:30 A.M. Sometimes the line was busy, and sometimes the mark answered and would be almost—hysterical."

Terrorism

A great scam for these tumultuous times is to turn your mark into a terrorist. Ginger from Tampa was bothered by local rowdies and hoodlums who terrorized her and her elderly brother. Her son suggested that since the neighborhood hooligans were acting like terrorists, they might as well get full recognition. He went to a hardware store and bought pieces of plumbing pipe and end caps.

"I stuffed some of the pipes with sand, drilled a small hole in the middle, and stuck in a 'fuse,' actually a piece of cord covered with glue. I put the end caps on. Then I put a few more of these 'bomb components,' including an empty black powder can in a paper bag," the son wrote.

"I planted this bag under the seat of one of the hoodlum's cars, then called police and reported terrorists driving that car and waving submachine guns around. Within an hour, the car was spotted, the young owner was rousted, his car was searched, and the fun was on. I also called local TV stations to tip them off, and one reporter actually showed up with a camera and shot film to use on the air. The parents were furious with their kid and didn't believe his plea of innocence anymore than the police did. It slowed the hoodlums down a lot because the police kept watching them after that."

We live during insane times, and a good trickster will take full advantage of this fact.

Toilets

Perhaps you are unhappy with some religious sect or establishment church. Find an especially disgusting toilet which is filled-to-overflowing unflushable, and thus churning with stomach-turning contents and odor. You will place neatly printed stick-on labels on the stall door. Each plaque reads:

DO NOT FLUSH
A (Name of Religion) BAPTISMAL FONT

It is great to do this in a hotel just as a group of visiting religious freaks from that particular persuasion are checking in for a convention. A friend of mine did this because of truly evil things the Mormon Church did to his wife. He printed his cards ending in "A MORMON BAPTISMAL FONT." He reports that when the Latter Day Saints came marching into the hotel and saw the stickers, they threatened the management with the wrath of Joseph Smith and His sidekick, God.

As an extra touch, my friend said he used a couple pens to scribble doodles and phone numbers on the stickers, added a few graffiti, wore down the edges, then smudged them . . . all to make the stickers appear that they'd been there for awhile. This would, of course, indicate the tacit approval of the hotel employees and management. It added to the impact a great deal, he said.

Utility Companies

Stop reading. Put this book down and think for a moment about the effect on your immediate life there at home if you were suddenly denied water or electricity. Who controls our electric power and our water supplies? Mostly, a monopoly known as a public utility controls these creature comforts. That fact makes stunts involving these utility companies work mightily to your advantage.

Several years ago, a nasty, nosey neighbor was hassling, prying and spying on a very nice person who read my first book and wrote to me about all this. After waiting awhile to avert suspicion, this reader visited the nasty neighbor's mailbox while that evil person was at work. Only the water company bill, and nothing else, was removed. At this point, the nasty neighbor became the mark.

This went on for several months. The dunning notices were also stolen. A cancellation of service notice was removed. A final notice was taken out. Then, one day, a water company crew arrived to shut off the mark's water. It took several dry days to straighten out the entire situation. This stunt didn't cure the neighbor's nasty habits, but it gave the reader a sense of getting back.

I should add that some folks who work for the U.S. Postal Monopoly regard "mail tampering" as a very serious federal offense. Be careful.

Vending Machines

A reader named Joe Morris has a profitable sense of humor about being ripped off by a vending machine. Joe says that so many people get ripped off so often that it's hard to find an innocent machine anymore. Here's his idea.

"I don't want to damage the machine, just the reputation of its owner. And, I want to get back my money and a little interest in return.

"All you need is a big wad of cotton, like the kind that comes in a roll at the drug store. Wrap a wire around it and stuff it up the coin return shaft in the machine, until the wire is just above the opening and can't be seen. The next day, come back, pull out your wire and receive a refund of the fullest kind."

Joe says this works only on the machines that don't have covers over the coin returns. He says it works like a charm on machines which drop the change right into the same tray as the product. But, clog just the coin shaft, not the product shaft. Otherwise . . . zero.

Here's a good question from S 'n' M of Ansonia, Connecticut. He wants to know why any trickster would spend good money on brass washers to rip off a newspaper vending machine. He has an easier way.

"Usually, there is a small hole on the tops of these machines. Stick a pin or something thin, strong, and sharp in there, push down, and pull on the door. It will open, and you'll have your paper."

Readers should note that some companies weld over or plug these holes for precisely this reason. But, there are other methods, like No. 14 brass washers.

VIP

We've all tried to get that always unavailable Very Important Person Who Can Solve Our Problem on the telephone. But that Important Person always is tied up, is in a meeting, or just stepped out of the office. So after you waste your time calling him or her in vain a few times, do it yet one more time.

This time come armed with the name of the chief executive officer of the company. Get that from the main switchboard operator. When the unavailable Very Important Person's flunky starts to give you the runaround again, sternly tell the flunky something like this:

"I didn't want to bring [use full name of chief executive] into this little matter. I thought your [use name of very important person here] could handle this him/herself. I guess not. Well, I'm calling [first name of chief executive] for a luncheon soon, and I can just ask him/her about this matter then."

No person wants the superior, especially the chief executive, to think that he/she is incapable of handling routine matters. Beyond that, the fact that you have namedropped adds a dimension few bureaucratic managers care to call as a bluff. It's easier and cheaper to finally talk to you—and satisfy you.

Visually Handicapped

This is a variation of that old film routine with W.C. Fields as a shopkeeper waiting on a blind man. You can use it to bamboozle those elected old pharts and their toadies who run your municipality as their own fiefdom. You and a friend enter their offices dressed in curious color and design variations, wearing dark glasses, carrying large white canes, and then you start bumping into things. Make demands that the minutes of local board meetings be provided in Braille and that all ordinances be so published.

If your community newspaper is like so many of this country, i.e., a publicity extension of the local merchants, with a Chamber of Commerce mentality, pull the same stunt in their offices. Demand a Braille edition. There is a lot of expensive equipment in newspaper offices, e.g., computer and video display terminals, TV sets, monitors, et cetera. A blind person and his cane can't be held responsible for this damage, especially if the newspaper people are insensitive to their needs. Ho, ho, ho. The only needs many newspaper people are sensitive to are those of the big advertisers.

Water Wells

People who live outside the lines of municipal services provide their own utilities, one of which is a water well. Normally, these wells are topped by a simple metal cap held in place by several set screws. It takes only a few minutes to loosen the screws, remove the cap, and dump a load of modest-sized roadkill down the well casing. Replace the cap and tighten the screws, and the mark will be none the wiser. For a while.

Water wells are usually purified once a year by adding a gallon of chlorine bleach to the well. This process also oxidizes the iron in the water, turning the liquid a dirty color. The water now stinks and tastes awful. To demolish the quality of your mark's water supply for at least a week, dump about fifteen gallons of bleach down the well.

Barfo Renchquist got his nickname as you might imagine. His favorite water-well trick is to eat all sorts of multi-colored greasy junk food, like pizza. He drinks a lot of beer, too. Primed and loaded, he is driven to the mark's water well. The well cap is removed, and Barfo positions himself over the well casing and pulls his trigger by sticking his finger down his throat. Barfo does his thing—all of it down the well. The well cap is replaced.

"It works best when they don't have too fine a filter on their pump and some of the small pieces of puke come out the house taps. A lot of the color, smell, and taste almost always comes through. It's a very demoralizing stunt," Barfo reports.

Weapons

According to L.T. from Mark Twain Land, a crossbow is a splendid weapon to use for creative revenge. My Twainian friend notes the crossbow may be used for silent attacks on domestic animals, breaking windows, putting holes in buildings or vehicles, or scaring the excrement out of a mark via a near miss. In some localities, crossbows are illegal, but then, so is marijuana.

There are lesser weapons. Thomas Bicipieu had an uncaring neighbor who allowed his large and uncivilized dogs to roam all over Thomas's property, leaving their large, unsightly and smelly calling cards all over the lawn, flowers, and garden. After several gentle, neighborly complaints, followed by a rather stiff telephone call, Thomas noticed no lessening of the doggie dung.

"I'll fight fire with spray, so to speak," he vowed.

With that, he took an empty spray bottle of the type used to squirt anticongestant up one's nose as in those horrible TV commercials. He made the opening a bit larger so it could be emptied faster. He filled it with fresh urine after a long, hard night of drinking beer and eating hard-boiled eggs.

Thomas began to make sneak attacks on his neighbor's automobile, spraying load after load into the car's interior as he passed by several times while walking his own leashed and trained dog. Thomas reports that in summer's heat, the stench of stale urine does wonders for the interior of a car . . . not to mention the fringe benefit of seat stains.

According to Mr. Bicipieu, this same weapon may be used to pay back merchants who have wronged you—especially clothing, food or furniture people. If you dare not walk into the store itself, you can always discharge a much larger vessel—say a quart or half gallon size container—into the air conditioner intake.

Dispensed properly, urine is wonderful stuff.

Wills

If you have a least-favorite friend, relative, or other family member you want to shame in front of the others, write him/her into your last will and testament. Simply instruct your attorney to include a codicil to the effect that "I bequeath all my yachts, silver plate, gold bullion and coins, foreign holdings, carriages, and aircraft to [name of mark]." Obviously, you had best not have any of those items, or you suddenly *become* the mark. This stunt is a blow from the grave. Maybe you won't know how it works. Maybe, though, you will. Is there revenge after death?

Women's Stores

This one works wonderfully well at those old line stores where people like your mother or a proper aunt buy their fancy clothes. You mount a small TV camera-like box on one of the top corners of the dressing cubicle where ladies try on their prospective purchases. Tape a small printed sign under the box, noting, "For Private Security Purposes Only, Do Not Be Alarmed." Sign the card with name of the store manager. Your printer made these signs for you.

If you wish to be even more ballsy, add the following message, too. "Mature security personnel destroy all photographs immediately if there is no evidence of retail theft." According to one field report this last sign blushed up storm that almost ended in a lawsuit against the store.

Why such a rotten trick? In an earlier case of mistaken identity, store security personnel had challenged a totally innocent woman, accusing her of being a shoplifter. They weren't going to let her go, up to and including the store manager, until she mentioned she was dating a local activist attorney—which was a bit of an exaggeration, because she knew him only as a social acquaintence.

Later, this young lady proceeded with the scam outlined above . . . much more fun than a real lawsuit. And, as she points out, when your settlement is outstanding laughter, you don't have to share an outrageous sum of it with some lawyer.

Zippers

Joe LaTorre suggests a bit of whimsical harassment that could have some real teeth in it. If you have to put up with someone who is appropriately annoying and who also wears a coat with a zipper, he offers an idea.

"Use a pair of pliers to firmly bend the right hand receiver (on a man's coat—reverse for women) just enough so the guide on the other side will not slip into the receiver. Don't leave plier marks, or bend it so much that it is noticeable; just enough so it won't work," Joe suggests.

He also says to be sure and talk to your mark while he or she is trying to get this zapped zipper to work. It makes things more frustrating, especially if you're putting on subtle pressure or acting semi-impatient. Joe calls it a minor irritant, but he says it causes true frustration. I like it.

About the Author

GEORGE HAYDUKE is a modern Robin Hood—a champion for those who are sick of letting bullies run roughshod over them—who has taken up the cause of victims and little guys everywhere. His other books include:

- *Advanced Backstabbing and Mudslinging Techniques*
- *Getting Even: The Complete Book of Dirty Tricks*
- *Getting Even 2: More Dirty Tricks From the Master of Revenge*
- *Make 'Em Pay: Ultimate Revenge Tactics From the Master Trickster*
- *Make My Day: Hayduke's Best Revenge Techniques for the Punks in Your Life*
- *Mayhem! From the Master of Malice*
- *Revenge: Don't Get Mad, Get Even*
- *Revenge Is Sweet: Dozens of Wicked Ways to Have the Last Laugh*
- *Revenge Tactics From the Master: Hardcore Hayduke*
- *Rightous Revenge: Getting Down to Getting Even*